The Art

of

Orchestration

Original MS Sketch by Debussy of Opening of Symphonic Suite *La Mer:* "De l'Aube à Midi sur la Mer."

By courtesy of the Sibley Music Library, Eastman School of Music, University of Rochester. Permission for reproduction authorized by Durand & Cie, Paris, France, and Elkan-Vogel Company, Inc., Philadelphia, copyright owners. (See Appendix, Ex. 14)

The
Art of Orchestration

PRINCIPLES OF TONE COLOR
IN MODERN SCORING

BERNARD ROGERS

Eastman School of Music
University of Rochester

NEW YORK

APPLETON-CENTURY-CROFTS, INC.

For the use of musical examples we are indebted to the publishers listed below. The page references are to this book.

Reprinted by permission of the copyright owner, Boosey and Hawkes, Inc.:
Bartok, *Piano Concerto* (pp. 129, 130)
Moussorgsky-Ravel, *Pictures at an Exhibition* (pp. 148-151, 179)
Stravinsky, *Chant du Rossignol* (p. 186)
Stravinsky, *Petrouchka* (pp. 65, 97, 174)

Used by permission of Enoch & Cie, Paris. Sole Western Hemisphere representatives: Southern Music Publishing Company, Inc., New York:
Chabrier, *Sous Bois,* from *Suite Pastorale* (p. 46)

Permission for reprint granted by copyright owners, Durand & Cie, Paris, and sole agents in the U.S.A., Elkan-Vogel Co., Inc., Philadelphia:
Debussy, *Ibéria* (pp. 19, 81) .
Debussy, *La Mer* (frontispiece, p. 182)
Dukas, *L'Apprenti Sorcier* (p. 175)
Ravel, *Mother Goose Suite* (p. 183)

Permission for reprint granted by Editions Jean Jobert, Paris, and Elkan-Vogel Co., Inc., Philadelphia, copyright owners:
Debussy, *Nuages* (p. 180)

Permission for reprint granted by Elkan-Vogel Co., Inc., Philadelphia, copyright owners:
Rogers, *The Passion* (p. 21)

Permission for reprint granted by Elkan-Vogel Co., Inc., Philadelphia:
Rogers, *Snow Queen* (p. 185)

TO

MY WIFE

MY MILDEST CRITIC

Theme and Variations

All art aspires to the condition of music.
—PATER

I believe that music returns the compliment embodied in Pater's phrase. The feeling of music flows through all the arts, and music comes refreshed from their touch.

My theme, with variations, is the special kinship of instruments and color: between their manipulation and the devices of painting. All composers feel the affinity, consciously or not. Were it necessary, one could offer great witnesses—Mozart, Beethoven, Berlioz, Liszt, Wagner, Strauss. They are but a few.

To orchestrate is to paint. Both arts enlist color and line as expressive means. In both, the sensuous ingredient sharpens and deepens the artist's thought.

Orchestration requires imagination, taste, and skill. It combines adventure and discipline. It is possible to define a perfect score: The right notes in the right places. That is the ideal—the shining standard of a Mozart. Lucidity is the highest prize of the orchestrator.

Part I of this book is devoted to a concise description of the present-day instrumental types. The latter continue to evolve, while the technique of players expands. The playing level described is that of a good professional.

I have ignored the history and genealogy of instruments; for the interested, there are copious sources of such material. Nor has space been found for instruments now extinct. Theirs is a decent desuetude. Let them repose.

The organ has not been discussed in these pages. It is not an "orchestral" instrument, and its marriage with the orchestra is usually one of convenience rather than of love.

A number of exercises, designed for the less experienced student, have been included. Transcription, or arranging, is a rewarding practice, and is a useful addition to original writing. But the student is urged to score his own music at an early stage.

The illustrations are drawn mainly from the last two centuries, using music which is readily accessible in score and performance. The extracts from my own music are designed to show certain personal or experimental procedures. Unless otherwise designated, references are to miniature-score editions.

This book is the result of long experience as composer and as teacher at the Eastman School of Music. It is addressed to the beginner as well as to the advanced student. And it is hoped that composers too will find some of the material stimulating—or provoking.

My thanks are due to Howard Hanson and the Eastman-Rochester Orchestra, who have over many years provided a hospitable shelter for my rather whimsical tonal ventures; also to Frederick Fennell, for his discerning interpretations of my chamber orchestra scores.

I am indebted to Carl Alette, Robert Lewis, Byron McCulloh, Lyndol Mitchell, Catherine Phelps, and Phyllis Saffron for assisting me to gather technical material.

B. R.

Contents

Part One
The Tonal Elements

CHAPTER I

The Palette

Strings, Winds, and Percussion are the basic instrumental values, resembling in principle the primary colors of light. We may compare them with the hues of pigment. (There is, of course, no literal correspondence; the phenomena of color differ in the spheres of light and sound.)

We shall set the tonal palette:

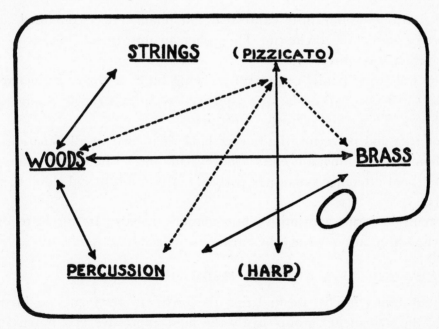

Pure colors (single families, solo types) are relatively transparent. Mixtures produce secondary shades and tints, more or less opaque. Mixing leads to neutrality—increasing grayness. Hence, doubling, especially at unison, should be used in moderation. The orchestrator must understand the properties of each tone color and group: its chemical characteristics (so to speak).

On the above palette the choirs have been linked by either solid or broken lines to show their affinities ("neighborliness") or antipathies. Thus, it appears that woodwinds mix readily with strings and brass and are friendly to percussion. Legato strings combine unwillingly with the brilliant brass (trumpet-trombone) or with the incisive tones of percussion. But note that horns form an exception: they afford a fine bridge color. Generally speaking, brass displays a somewhat aloof temper.

Plucked strings—including the harp—form an outlying group, quasi-percussive in effect. These associate freely with all winds and percussion. Also related to percussion are piano, celesta, and harpsichord. Tremolando and other novel methods of string playing create another link with the several choirs.

Strings and winds form the lyric-harmonic elements. They bear the true musical burden, as opposed to percussion, whose rôle—largely rhythmic and coloristic—is occasional.

THE FOUR CHOIRS

The strings—wonderfully expressive and pliant—are a contained unit: an orchestra within the orchestra. They offer an unsurpassed means of variety and technical resource.

The woodwind family is diversified, being built of three distinctive types. These small pure voices, lacking assertiveness, must struggle against massive neighbors. They need sensitive treatment.

Compact and powerful, the brasses hold their own in all situations. They are homogeneous, magnificently sonorous and vital, whether in solo or group action. Bold utterance suits them perfectly. Mutes dilute and cloud their clear colors.

Percussion forms a primitive but complex palette. Its hues are dry and detached, stinging or savage by turn.

WOODWINDS AS A UNITING MEDIUM

Summarizing briefly, we find that the orchestra rests on two broad supports: the string-wind group—easily the most expressive and important—and the rhythmic-coloristic percussion. Woods combine fluently with all choirs. Brasses show some reluctance to mix with bowed strings, though they consort well with woods and percussion. Strings form the chief lyric-harmonic element, capable unaided of sustaining the musical idea for considerable periods.

It is important to remember the versatile nature of the woodwinds. They facilitate a plastic blend of strings and brass, reconciling basic antagonisms between those groups.

We may note also that compact mixtures generally result from the union of instruments of related pitch range. The latter frequently combine in harmonic functions. Instruments widely separated in range introduce curious contradictions of color, harmonically and melodically.

Percussion imparts strong lights and shadows, besides accents and effects of atmosphere. Its psychological suggestion is immediate.

GROUPINGS ON THE PALETTE

The grand orchestral palette may now be separated into its components. Thus we arrive at groupings which represent a palette for each choir, and—to carry the process still further—a spectrum for each instrument. The palette is disclosed as a wide array of subtly modulated hues and shades.

Three general values are present, agreeing roughly with the individual registers—deep (dark), medium (neutral), high (bright). In the case of stringed instruments, the four individual strings of each type present characteristic colors that flow smoothly into their neighbors. Adjacent strings display least differences; separated strings present stronger contrasts.

TWO CATEGORIES

Reverting to the full palette, we find a broad division between instruments of prevailingly dark or bright suggestion. (Instruments in brackets have an exceptional color range.)

Bright	Dark
Violin	Viola
[Cello]	[Cello]
Piccolo	Double bass
Flute	Oboe
[Clarinet]	English horn
Trumpet	[Clarinet]
[Tenor trombone]	Bass clarinet
Small percussion	Bassoon
	Double bassoon
	Horn
	[Tenor trombone]
	Bass trombone
	Tuba
	Large percussion

(This division is arbitrary; it is based on personal impression.)

As a general principle, instruments mix freely with others found in the same category. There is, however, considerable agreement between instruments of both categories, especially those of comparable pitch range. As will be seen later, instruments of each family share a certain common gamut; herein lies a simple means of achieving variety and distinction of timbre.

The terms *bright* and *dark* are used in a relative sense. All instruments are relatively tense and clear in their acute registers, somber in the deep areas.

CHAPTER II

The Sovereign Strings

The strings have long held power in the orchestral kingdom. But the last century has seen their rule relaxed. The emergence of the Romantic-Nationalist schools, led by such pioneers as Berlioz, Liszt, Glinka, and Wagner, has brought elements of democracy. Winds and percussion have been enfranchised; the hegemony of the strings has given place to a benign leadership. The process of liberation was strongly assisted by the addition of valves to the brass group and by mechanical refinements among the woods.

It is easy to understand the influence retained by the strings. They are uniquely endowed. To a commanding technique they add the finest shades of expression. Their great cohesive powers enable the members to unite or separate at will; meanwhile the individual types retain strong identity.

BASIC TECHNIQUE

The basic technique of the strings is one of "position." At all times the player (violinist or violist) commands a full two octaves in each position. We show the note series in the first two positions of the violin. The technique of the other stringed instruments rests on a related principle:

EXAMPLE 1

As the player moves his left hand up the fingerboard, the series ascends. The notes in each position may be played in any spelling, with or without accidentals. It is somewhat unusual to write above the ninth position.[1] Players tend to favor the odd-numbered positions.

It will be seen that the foundation of string technique rests on scale—diatonic or chromatic. But arpeggios are well within the string means. Thus two octaves are available in any given position, the bow merely moving from one string to another (preferably adjacent) when a skip demands. Position-change, however, requires a shift of the left hand.

Passage work lying in a single position is always favorable. But skipping a string *in rapid passages* should be avoided:

EXAMPLE 1*a*

This passage involves at once a wide change of position and the skipping of (two) strings.

Here no change of position or string is needed; the fifth note is produced as an artificial harmonic on the G-string (see discussion of Harmonics on pages 17 to 18). The two-octave skip would necessitate a movement of the arm if taken on the piano:

EXAMPLE 1*b*

A figure involving movement of the arm in piano technique may require no left-hand shift at all for the string player—merely a change of string. This is obviously true of passages which lie in the same position (see Ex. 1*b*). Hence, string passages should never be judged on the basis of piano problems. Players

[1] The student should continue the sequence up to and including the thirteenth position. He will thus have a chart for future reference. Similar charts, transposed, should be made for the larger stringed instruments, up to the ninth position. Such charts should note altered fingerings, which will be described later.

often adopt a change of position to secure variety of tone color or for other expressive objectives.

CHROMATICS

In the older technique, the same finger was generally employed for a note and its chromatic inflections, thereby producing a slight slide or *portamento*. Present-day style employs different fingers. Here is one fingering:

EXAMPLE 2

Other fingerings are available, but the one given involves a minimum of *portamento*.

Where well-defined chromatic intonation is desired, write "with clarity" over the passage.

RANGES OF THE STRING FAMILY

The ranges of the string group are spacious.

EXAMPLE 3

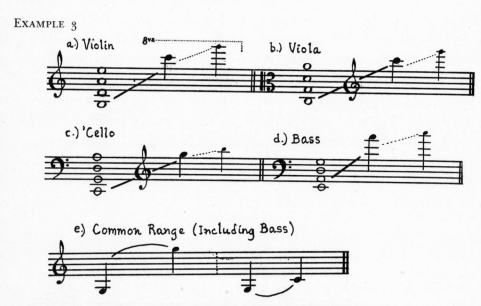

The Bass always sounds an octave below written notes.

(Open strings are shown in white note-heads.)

These ranges are substantially extended (upward) through the use of harmonics. (For younger players the limits shown above should be lowered a fourth.)

The student should memorize the common range (e). Within this territory the crossing of instruments becomes richly expressive in lyric passages. Imagine the opening motive of *Tristan* assigned to the violins or violas instead of to the poignant tint of the cello's A-string! Or a substitute for the latter color in the Wolf Glen music of *Der Freischütz* (page 3 of Overture). Passages confided to a particular string yield a pure, intense, and even color. They should not be excessive in range: a twelfth is feasible, a tenth is safer. Avoid over-use of this device; it soon wears thin.

A powerful example of this coloring is quoted in the Appendix (No. 11) from the Moussorgsky-Ravel *Pictures at an Exhibition*. The violins are taken up a tenth (B-flat) on the G-string. A famous usage is the beginning of the development section of Tchaikovsky's Sixth Symphony, savage and sonorous in character.

EXPRESSIVE SCOPE

Strings can assume all expressive rôles. And—unlike the winds—they possess individual harmonic possibilities, thanks to their power of stopping chords. The dynamic scale is a subtle one, embracing all shades of volume and intensity. (Present references are mainly to the violin, but also apply to the other strings.)

The four violin strings show decisive contrasts. The lowest (G) is somber and vibrant (in *forte*). The highest string (E) is radiant and penetrating. The middle strings (A and D) are sober in color, admirable for intimate expression or subdued backgrounds. Note that the third (D) string has less power and impact than the others. When a robust, vibrant character is desired, a passage in this area should be marked *Sul G*. On the fourth string, rhythmic figures such as ostinati in all dynamics are tellingly effective. Also idiomatic and striking is a wide shift of register (across strings):

EXAMPLE 4

Weber: Overture to *Oberon*

(Détaché bowing)

In the highest positions, difficulties of intonation present a serious problem. Here discretion is the watchword. Simple passages, especially of diatonic and sequential character, which lie "under the hand" in one or two positions, are recommended. In these altitudes avoid fussy chromatic writing, sudden wide changes of position, and angular tone patterns. The pedal (sustained tone) is clear and telling in high registers, full and powerful on low strings.

BOWING [2]

Bowing is the stringed instrument's way of breathing. Thus, bowing technique, subtly linked with expression, is of cardinal importance in string writing. The non-string player should consult a seasoned orchestral performer; only through detailed advice and demonstration can this problem be understood. Also essential is intent study of string parts in score and performance.

The bow strokes are:

> Legato
> Staccato
> Détaché [3] (at various portions of the bow)
> Spiccato (thrown bow)
> Saltando
> Portato (Louré)
> Hammer-stroke (martellato) at point or heel
> Group bowings

These are employed to model phrase units and rhythmic fragments, and to impart force, distinction, and shading. For instance, a group of down-bows in deliberate tempo (which cannot be played effectively in rapid succession) lends bold emphasis.

Down-bow is a positive stroke, quasi-masculine, apposite for energetic effect and for chord stopping. But this stroke can also be adapted to more subtle suggestion. (It is not synonymous with *down-beat*.)

Up-bow is less vigorous; it is more intimate in nature, and is especially telling for crescendo. It is essentially an expressive stroke, often applied to the up-beat.

We illustrate some standard bowings:

Détaché: A forceful long-bow, suitable for most tempi.

[2] For an illuminating discussion of bow technique, including a rare analysis of bow-and-finger accent, consult Hermann Scherchen's *Handbook of Conducting* (London: Oxford University Press, Humphrey Milford, 1933). This treatise, despite its title, is rich in suggestions for the composer.

[3] In the true sense, détaché, despite its connotation, is a species of broad *legato* stroke; the tones are subtly separated or delicately connected. (The first two notes of Ex. 4 would be played as a powerful détaché.)

EXAMPLE 4*a*

Staccato: May be a group of light notes under a single bow, or may be indicated by dots without slurs.

EXAMPLE 4*b*

Group staccato: A frequent bowing, effective for rhythmic patterns.

EXAMPLE 4*c*

Spiccato: Resembles staccato, but the bow is thrown on the string. An elastic bounding stroke. Always indicate in the part.

EXAMPLE 4*d*

Martellato: As its name implies, a hammered stroke, available in any part of the bow. In *forte* it is harsh and powerful when played at heel (*du talon*). Unsuited to very rapid tempi.

EXAMPLE 4*e*

Saltando: The bow is allowed to bound, picking up a small group of notes. Effective for background or dance rhythms. Not suited to strong dynamics (a down-bow effect).

EXAMPLE 4f

Louré (portato): An expressive, lingering stroke, often up-bow. Excellent for marking certain moments of a subject, or for italicizing motives in sequence.

EXAMPLE 4g

COLOR, DYNAMICS, AND BOWING

One should study the subtle color variations that result when the bow is used at the tip, center, or heel. Note that a change of bow does not necessarily imply an accent: the "joint" can be smoothly sealed (see footnote on page 11). And observe that the bow must travel faster for a *forte* than for a *piano*. Hence, in strong dynamics fewer notes are given to a single bow. Composers sometimes place a long slur over a phrase; this indicates the over-all modeling, within which the bow-frame work is defined.

CHORD STOPPING

Chord stopping is another complex subject. Most double stops, up to and including the octave, are practical, even without open string, if not placed extremely high (E above the staff as top note of the octave). Multiple-note stops are best set in open position (fifths, sixths, or sevenths). Perfect fifths are stopped with a single finger; their intonation is not dependable. Nor is the intonation of octaves quite reliable. Full chords sound tame in *piano,* and are played usually down-bow. They should be written not in quick succession; separated by brief rests, their defiant stroke in *forte* is immensely effective. Here is a dramatic string accent-chord (pizzicato) from the *Tristan* Prelude:

EXAMPLE 5

Wagner: *Prelude to Tristan and
Isolde* (page 2)

When several notes must be played simultaneously by one section of strings, divided strings (*Divisi*) yield superior tone and intonation; they are always preferable to double or multiple stops for expressive passages.

Chord figuration is a fine textural resource, easy and useful at moderate altitudes either legato or staccato. (All patterns that can be played as chords can be performed in arpeggio style.) Among a host of examples for reference we cite the "Magic Fire" scene from *Die Walküre,* the opening of *En Saga* of Sibelius—a most elaborate pattern of dispersed chords—and *España* of Chabrier, pages 12 to 16, inclusive. The presence of open strings slightly disturbs tone balance but facilitates chord problems and is recommended. We emphasize that the chord particles are best arranged in open position.

PIZZICATO

This is a resource of unique value. (It is worth noting that, except for the harp, pizzicato is the sole plectral means normally used in the symphony orchestra. Jazz bands—never snobbish—shrewdly conscript guitar, banjo, and—rarely—harpsichord.)

Pizzicato brings a valuable liaison between strings and the other choirs, especially percussion. The color is glittering, though somewhat dry, in the higher positions. Far up on the E-string, it suggests the crisp rattle of hailstones:

EXAMPLE 6

Tchaikovsky: Sixth Symphony (page 162)

Like bowed chords, pizzicato stops should not be written in very rapid succession, although these *can* be played with an up-and-down motion, the violin (or viola) being held somewhat like a guitar. Berlioz prescribes a guitarlike procedure in his solo of Mephistopheles *(Damnation of Faust)*; the second violins and violas are directed to use the thumb for their four-note arpeggios.

Chords may be played either *piano* or *forte*; the latter dynamic is more effective (See Ex. 5). Protracted pizzicato is fatiguing. The *Scherzo* of Tchaikovsky's Fourth Symphony is a famous example of continued pizzicato. Another charming example occurs in the *Larghetto* of Prokofieff's *Classical* Symphony. In any case, over-use soon sounds mannered.

Pizzicato passages which pass from one group to another have an excellent effect, both for scales and arpeggios. The strings are usually plucked with a single finger. (Some players practice a double-finger technique.) Played thus, pizzicato cannot go too rapidly: eighth notes in an Allegro are feasible.

Occasional *brief* passages at rapid pace may be given to the low stringed instruments. Their effect is dramatic, although apt to sound clouded (Storm section from Beethoven's *Pastoral* Symphony). All large instruments speak less clearly than their small companions. A single plucked note, soft or loud, from the deep strings is curiously compelling (see page 3 of *Der Freischütz* Overture).

PIZZICATO VARIANTS

Modern variants are the lifted- and slapped-string pizzicato. For the former —used in *forte*—the string is raised and made to strike the fingerboard with whiplike effect. Bartok employs it in his Divertimento for Strings. (See page 2 of that score.) Rare (although used by Beethoven) is the pizzicato *portamento*; the player slides from the stopped note while the plucked string is vibrating. A weak resource unless the string section is a large one.

Written optionally:

EXAMPLE 7

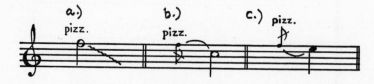

Virtually unknown is the use of the fingernail for pizzicato, practicable only at very deliberate tempo. The sound is sharply metallic, especially brilliant when used on an open string. Another rare device is the pizzicato tremolo, in Italian, *bisbigliando*. It may be used for chords, the strings being strummed with the fleshy part of the fingers. Elgar employs this method during the cadenza of his Violin Concerto, using half of the violins, violas, and cellos only, playing *pianissimo*.

Occasionally used is the left-hand pizzicato, available on open strings. It is indicated by a cross over the note. (An example from Glazounoff is given at the end of this chapter.)

HARMONICS

Harmonics extend the string spectrum upward with delicate shadings which recall the soft high tones of small woodwinds. Divided strings in harmonics are of ethereal radiance in *piano*. In *forte* they are clear and whistling, effective for brilliant accents. Five natural harmonics are generally used: octave, twelfth, double-octave, double-octave plus major third, double-octave plus perfect fifth. They may be notated at actual pitch with a small circle over the note, or a diamond-shaped note may be written to show the *fingering* with an ordinary note above to indicate actual sound.

Artificial harmonics are produced by stopping with the first finger and lightly touching the string a *perfect fourth* higher with fourth finger. This is the only artificial harmonic in general use for orchestra. Note that the sound is two octaves above the *stopped* note.

Notation of natural and artificial harmonics:

EXAMPLE 8

Harmonics have the clearest effect on the two upper strings of each instrument, while on the lower two they have a fine, veiled timbre.

Played pizzicato—a rare device—harmonics recall the sound of tiny, distant bells. (They should not be written for younger players.)

The use of harmonics should be restricted, as should all novel devices. Nor should they be written in rapid succession. Berlioz provides a fine example (*Queen Mab* Scherzo) of three-part chords combining natural and artificial harmonics:

EXAMPLE 9

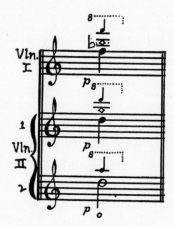

A brilliant modern effect is the bowed glissando starting from an open string and ending with a natural harmonic on the same string:

EXAMPLE 10

TREMOLO

Tremolo is generally used at moments of agitation. A rhetorical device, tremolo is most effective on the first and fourth strings. It sounds mediocre at *mezzoforte*. Time and usage have been enemies of the tremolo. But the shuddering quality produced in the deepest strings retains much of its strange appeal. At the crest of a climax, a high, forceful tremolo seems to set fire to the orchestral fabric. Note also the effect of tremolo at different portions of the bow.

Here is a sensitive use of tremolo *sul tasto,* from Debussy's *Ibéria.* Eight first-violins are divided in four parts; thirds doubled at the octave change register at each bar. They produce a subdued shimmering:

EXAMPLE 11

Debussy: *Ibéria* (page 22)

The fingered tremolo is actually an expanded trill. It should not exceed a fourth on small strings or a major third on cello, except in high positions. Wider intervals must be played on adjacent strings, and are less effective. Its murmuring effect is magical in *pianissimo*. Debussy and Ravel have made fine use of this device.

Both bowed and fingered tremolo may be used simultaneously in divided strings. They are notated:

EXAMPLE 12

a. Bowed tremolo.

b. Fingered tremolo; equivalent to half-note value.

Tremolo is essentially a massed string resource, ineffectual for solo instruments.

The trill is rarely written on the *open* fourth string,[4] nor is it practical in extremely high altitudes. For the half-tone trill it is best not to exceed the ninth position, as the space between each pitch becomes rather small for pure intonation.

[4] Unless it is unavoidable, as in the case of the open fourth string, players do not trill on open strings.

MUTES

Mutes greatly reduce the resonance. They impart a veiled, hushed quality to the string choirs. In *forte* the sound is hauntingly strange and intense; in *piano,* remote and poetic. For a vivid example of the former, see "Ase's Death" from the *Peer Gynt* music (quoted on page 95); or the *Adagietto* from the first *Arlésienne* Suite of Bizet (note the somber viola pedal on open C-string). Further, the passage for eight muted violins in Weber's *Euryanthe* Overture, and the moment in Act II of *Tosca* when the heroine sees the knife.

Lovely as the effect of mutes can be, they are perhaps better avoided for passages of sentimental nature.

It is important to allow a few bars' rest to affix mutes; their removal needs only a few beats. As soon as the passage using mutes is concluded, the direction *Senza sordini* should be given.

EXCEPTIONAL MEANS

Among the unusual methods of bowing, recent scores have often employed the *sul ponticello* (on the bridge) and *sul tasto* (over the fingerboard). They should be discreetly used as marginal color shades. The former is essentially a tremolo resource. Its sound is glassy (painful in *forte*) in the higher strings, harshly metallic on the lower. It can be used spiccato with interesting results. Played pizzicato, the sound is dry and banjo-like.

Sul tasto is a more musical means. The tone becomes darker and more veiled (and vague) as the bow moves further toward the fingerboard. Various degrees of *sul tasto* are thus possible.[5] Beautifully expressive, the color recalls that of lightly muted strings. It is less practical for viola and cello, and is not used for Basses.

Col legno (with the wood of the bow) is a coloristic device, producing a dry, clattering effect. When the bow is *half turned,* so that both hair and wood engage the string, a rustling sound results. Used spiccato (as it often is) the effect is striking. Short chord strokes have a quasi-percussive suggestion, but lack power. In tremolo, *col legno* sounds paltry: there is more scratch than pitch. The player will not care to scrape the varnish from his bow in this fashion. Bass players refuse to use it.

---

[5] Players and conductors rarely avail themselves of the shadings produced by using various areas of the fingerboard.

VIBRATO AND NONVIBRATO

Vibrato is the life-giving means of string playing. Its application lies in the domain of feeling and taste, and is a wholly subjective matter.

Nonvibrato is occasionally prescribed. It adds a cool, withdrawn suggestion to the normal string palette. Here is a twelve-tone chord from the author's *Passion*: the sound is strangely "white" and disembodied.

EXAMPLE 13

Rogers: *Passion* (page 168, large score)

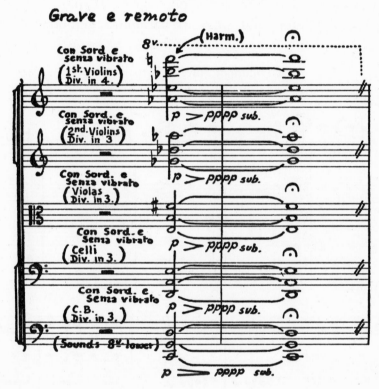

This chord occurs at the moment of Christ's death. It attempts to convey a feeling of pervading vacuum. The sound is utterly consonant.

SOLO STRINGS

The occasional use of solo strings is touchingly expressive, and contrasts curiously with the sound of the full choir. (Fine examples are frequent: see Debussy's *Afternoon of a Faun,* the early pages of Strauss's *Don Quixote,* and Ravel's *Mother Goose.)* Avoid solo string passages in music of a sentimental cast.

RHYTHMIC VARIETY

Almost unlimited are the rhythmic possibilities of the strings. The bow can be controlled at all speeds, while rhythmic patterns can be crisply delineated. Regular rhythmic patterns are always most successful. Change of bow *can* impart accent, although in cantabile the change of direction may be made imperceptibly. Some conductors prefer to have the players of a section employ individual bowings for long legato lines.

From Glazounoff's Novelettes for string quartet, we quote an example showing various bowings, stoppings, pizzicati, harmonics, and other devices:

EXAMPLE 14

Glazounoff: Novelettes (page 16)

(In the last bar the cello plays the pizzicato D with the left hand; it is an open string.)

EXERCISES

Write a number of passages for grouped violins, using different tempi, bowings, and so on. Include all details such as dynamics, staccato, phrasing.

Compose passages confined to an individual string, not exceeding a twelfth in range.

Employ all types of stopping and figuration, and invent rhythmic patterns as background effects.

Show use of natural and artificial harmonics.

Include passages for plucked strings, using single notes and chords.

Consider effect of tempo and dynamics on bowing.

The study of standard violin literature, including concertos, will be helpful; but it should not be forgotten that the virtuoso solo style is inappropriate in the sphere of orchestral writing.

CHAPTER III

The String Ensemble

QUALITIES OF THE DEEPER STRINGS

The strings form a medium capable of all shades of musical expression, Before discussing their use in ensemble, the viola, cello, and bass will be briefly considered.

THE VIOLA

The viola provides a true alto color. Indispensable for background functions, its warm tone is memorable at lyrical moments. Its defects—technical and tonal—change in curious fashion into virtues. The viola is decidedly not a "large violin"; in fact, it is usually built too small for its pitch range. Its accent is poetic and melancholy: the pervading pessimism borders on monotony.

The tone is thicker than that of the violin and somewhat husky, the articulation less clear and defined, while the bowing has a heavier character and needs more frequent changes. Less elastic and responsive than its smaller brother, the viola demands slightly more deliberate pacing.

The grave tones of the fourth string are weighty, harshly vibrant in *forte,* solemn and somber in *piano*. In rhythmic patterns—especially ostinato—the deepest string acquires a haunting, almost hypnotic quality. Spiccato does not emerge too clearly from this string.

The following extract from Rimsky-Korsakoff's *Sadko* shows a characteristic motive, legato, placed in the grave register. The bowing defines the motive outline. The written low B-sharp is enharmonic equivalent of the open C-string, and is so played. Only the string parts are quoted: in the full score they are doubled by winds and chorus.

EXAMPLE 14*a*

Rimsky-Korsakoff: *Sadko* (No. 1248)

The middle strings, in pitch equal to the G and D of the violin, are quite different in character. Their color is sere—admirable for both background and lyricism. They are consistently useful. But their reticence and—so to speak—anonymity frequently tempt over-use. These middle strings as solo media can be beautiful indeed.

The plaintive A-string has a penetrating, almost querulous, suggestion. It should not be over-used; in general, very high writing is best avoided for viola. (In its higher register the instrument should be treated as the *octave* relative of the violin; the seventh position is sufficient in most cases.) Mainly, the alto clef is used; avoid the treble clef unless a passage lies in the high register for several bars. Players prefer to remain in one clef for a period.

BLENDING PROPERTIES

The viola is undoubtedly one of the most useful instruments of the orchestra. Its propensity for blending with almost all colors often leads to monotony. Guard against this error.

As harmonic agent, the viola has unique value. Its color—at once rich and sober—forms fine background shades without dominating the ensemble.

Stops offer problems similar to those of the violin; they are slightly more taxing. It is well to avoid double-stops involving the perfect fourth and fifth. Cross-the-strings arpeggios are excellent in effect and are commonly used for accompanying formulas, either bowed or pizzicato. Write them in open position. The viola's tremolo has more substance than that of the violin and has an awesome suggestion when played on the fourth string. Repeated notes or rhythmic figures are invariably successful; again the fourth string imparts remarkable colorings. (See Ex. 14^a.)

The pizzicato has fine substance and is frequently employed.

It should be remembered that the viola responds less freely than the violin; thus it lacks the dazzling fluency of the latter. The mute profoundly changes the viola's character. Its tone becomes brooding, withdrawn, and mysterious, with a curious suggestion of distant horn color.

THE CELLO

Nobly endowed, both musically and technically, the cello carries out all functions in the tenor-bass range. Its versatility exceeds that of the viola while challenging that of the violin. The cello's sweeping compass and poignantly expressive tone join with a high degree of technical fluency. The luscious sound of its first string has led to abuse. Ration this rich resource.

The middle strings are flowing and suave, contemplative or tender, while the sonorous C-string affords a substantial bass in quiet passages. Rapid writing in the deep register is apt to be indistinct; although brief, characteristic figures are of admirable effect. (See fugal subject after No. 1; Prelude to Puccini's *Madama Butterfly*.) Accompaniment formulas are commonly employed; they are extremely useful and are easily playable in open patterns (fifths and sixths). This is illustrated in Example 14b.

The cello arpeggios, doubled by viola playing other chord-particles, lie well under the hand.

EXAMPLE 14*b*

Rimsky-Korsakoff: *Scheherazade* (page 38)

On the G-string the notes on the bass staff from D up to G, inclusive, lack color. They may be played on the D-string, or doubled by violas, when a full, dark color results. As with the other instruments, leaps across strings in rapid tempo are somewhat hazardous.

Multiple-stopping is often used and is excellent for broad, decisive accents. Avoid sudden leaps to extremely high notes. A brief rest before a big change of register is helpful.

The cello's range is large—a full three and one-half octaves—and the high notes emerge with fine effect. For the top register the player uses a "thumb" position, which facilitates the production of these notes. About two octaves above the open A-string are thus made available. But pure intonation in extremely high positions can be secured only from mature performers. For solo cello a total four-octave range may be employed. (See the score of Strauss's *Don Quixote*.)

Harmonics are easy, "speak" with fine clarity, and provide a valuable extension of the normal color range. Both natural and artificial varieties are freely available.

FINGERING

In the lower positions the cellist can stretch only a major third between first and fourth fingers. Skips of a fourth are thus less idiomatic than on the violin or viola; they present no serious problem, although superimposed fourths are better avoided. Chromatic scales are taken with separate fingers; their sound is crisp and precise.

Uniquely valuable is the cello pizzicato. It has more substance than that of the smaller strings, and combines elasticity and resonance. Its sound is full without heaviness, excellent for subdued passages, for brightening outlines (in upper register), or for powerful accents. It is well to limit the range to an octave above the A-string; above that point the sound soon "dries out." Pizzicato chords, which should be separated with rests, are extremely sonorous and colorful.

Like the viola, the cello offers such a variety of values that it is well to guard against its over-use. Three clefs are used: bass, tenor, and treble. Do not skip from clef to clef; it is better to write a few leger lines.

THE BASS

The Bass [1]—as we shall henceforth call the deepest string instrument—provides the foundation of the string choir. Because of its limited color range and technical restrictions, it needs careful use. Its dense, turbid quality brings weight and power, but the threat of monotony is ever present. The psychological effect of the Bass is profound. Its result is to darken the tonal setting—to cast shadow, never light.

Calculate its entrances and exits, and note the striking effect when, after an absence, the Bass returns with a thematic fragment. Few instruments gain so much from the presence of rests. The Bass is an instrument of drama.

While capable of swift movement, its true rôle is to provide a strong pedestal for the harmonic or lyric structure. The tone is thick, dark, and tense, mixing well with deep woods, horns, and tuba, as well as with cellos. Deliberate passages suit it well, and great power results from strong thrusts of its stubby bow.

Avoid wide changes of position, except for rare occasions. In the lower positions the player can stretch only a major second between first and fourth fingers. But scale designs can be dispatched with surprising speed, at the expense of clarity in the lower half of the compass. (See the *Scherzo* of Beethoven's Fifth Symphony.) Low trills are murky, too strongly marked for general use. The larger orchestras include a few Basses with a keyed extension permitting the player to reach low C (an octave below the cello fourth string). These deep notes are thick and slightly vague in pitch, useful mainly in soft dynamics and for held tones.

MONOTONY OF DEEP REGISTER

The ancient practice of octave doubling with cello, while acoustically excellent, should not be regarded as a stock resource. Use it intelligently, and remember that it is habit forming. The fact that the Bass is written an octave *above its sounding pitch,* often leads the student to overemploy the lower reg-

---

[1] The word *Bass*—with a capital letter—will be used to refer to the deepest of the strings.

ister. The effect of a giant-in-the-earth soon grows wearisome. The instrument's practical range (two-and-one-half octaves) offers sufficient chance for color change. But actually the Bass's sound is heavily somber, moving from black to shades of gray. The pizzicato is immensely effective; it can be produced at considerable speed, but should be deliberate in the lowest octave. The Bass bow is comparatively short, needing frequent changes of direction.

Double-stops are impractical on the Bass; they are better avoided even when an open string is available. Harmonics are clear and strong, but only the natural variety should be used.

THE STRING ORCHESTRA

The student should proceed to use the combined strings in a variety of musical tasks. A few basic principles are outlined here. He should aim for clarity: purity of part writing and rhythmic distinction are essential. Texture —varied and clear—is of cardinal importance. Good musical thinking is the first ingredient of good scoring.

ANATOMY OF THE STRING SCORE

The string picture displays lights and depths, peaks and valleys. Like an etching, its success rests on a striking disposal of a few masses carried out in related tones. String writing uses a variety of part-schemes; while four-voice writing is commonly employed, relief and variety result from the play of textures. Two- and three-part writing is a welcome alternative.[2] A single part may sustain the thought for brief periods, while five parts are occasionally used in more complex schemes. String quartets, though more slender in style, offer valuable clues. (See example at end of Chapter II.) But never confuse the style of string orchestra with that of the string quartet.

Use extreme ranges sparingly and with purpose. The composer must plan ahead, considering always the form and the need of contrast. *Scoring should serve musical structure.*

Departures from the normal, such as crossing of parts, bring intensified color. They must be used in moderation. The instruments should share the musical interest. The old-style "walking part" of the second violin has long since been raised to the dignity of a "speaking part." No group must commandeer the thematic interest. The bass part (of the harmony) should be ex-

[2] Mozart often uses a three-part scheme, and always with crystalline effect.

pressive while avoiding overactivity. Guard against monotony of register. Do not write consistently *on the staff* for any instrument.

SPACING

Differentiate between real and apparent parts. Consistent octave-doubling does not add a true voice; it is merely an effect of color. For the present, confine such doublings to soprano and bass parts. (But beware of habitual bass octaves. They point straight to monotony.) Octave-doubled alto and tenor tend to thickness. Keep soprano and bass lines clear of the middle strands; although alto and tenor may cross one another freely for expressive effect. Experience will justify exceptional practices. Doublings should serve a musical end, such as emphasis and color variation.

Close position among the three upper voices is favorable, but must not become habitual. The bass may be spaced at some distance from the tenor, when the musical line demands.

For chord effects, full (close) writing sounds well in *forte*. Open position is possible at all dynamic levels. In *piano,* this spacing yields textures of fine transparency.

Among the deeper instruments, close writing presents definite hazards. Beware of this common error except for special purposes. Complex patterns and overactivity in the low areas sound muddy unless handled with unusual skill.

DOUBLINGS

Unison doublings have a full, robust effect. First and second violins combine well at moments of broad expression. Mixture of viola and cello results in a strong, warm color (see *Andante* of Beethoven's Fifth Symphony). When the violas are using their C-string they are likely to predominate; while cellos take command when their first string is in action. Unison of all strings, except Basses, has great power and intensity. Its use is gravely impressive.

A superb example of octave doubling is found in the slow movement of Beethoven's Fourth Piano Concerto. The massed strings carry on a strangely dramatic dialogue with the solo instrument.

Basses are occasionally used independently. This is a poor procedure; they have a much clearer effect when doubled with a few cellos. They should rarely go above the cello part.

First violins often divide by octaves when a passage lies extremely high. Here the under-violins lend definition to the upper octave. For ultra-high writing a few violins suffice, especially in soft dynamics, if doubled an octave below by the remainder of the group. Additional suggestions for texture are given in later chapters.

Rests bring light and air to the fabric. Their importance cannot be over-emphasized. They define motives and phrases, clarify structure, and bring new shades to the color scheme, besides giving relief to the players.

Simple keys are easier and more resonant, owing to the open strings they afford. (The law of sympathetic vibration is always at work.) Note the tonalities employed by the Classic masters, and also the fact that they rarely exceed the fifth position in height.

The feeling of Song should permeate musical thinking.[3] Conceive of the instruments as voices; feel each part as a singing voice. Recall that the strings provide an ideal polyphonic medium—despite their kinship in color—and that polyphony is the noblest means of expression.

EXERCISES

The exercises which follow are planned for the inexperienced student. They should be supplemented with original writing for string orchestra.

As a preliminary, study a group of Classic string quartets and quintets, observing all details. Score reading should begin here and should be continually practised, mentally and at the piano. The four common clefs should be mastered. Reading of quartets, if faithfully pursued, will form a good basis for later work with full score. (Avoid focusing on the first violin part.)

Score a few Bach chorales, each in two ways. (See subjoined examples.)

Score Nos. 2, 9, 17, and 23 from Schumann's *Album for the Young*.

Score the Sonata in G major, Op. 49, No. 2, of Beethoven.

Using piano score, arrange portions of Grieg's *Holberg* Suite, finally comparing your version with the original string score.

Additional works for study:

> Bach, Concerto for Two Violins in D minor
> Mozart, *Eine Kleine Nachtmusik*
> Grieg, *Two Elegiac Pieces*
> Tchaikovsky, Serenade in C
> Arensky, *Variations on a Theme by Tchaikovsky*
> Vaughan Williams, *Fantasy on a Theme by Tallis*

[3] "To sing is the life function of music. Where there is no singing, the forms of music become distorted and they move in a senseless time-order imposed from without." Hermann Scherchen, *Handbook of Conducting* (London: Oxford University Press, Humphrey Milford, 1933).

Hanson, String Quartet
Honegger, String Symphony
William Schuman, String Symphony
Bartók, Divertimento for String Orchestra
Barber, *Adagio*

Here are two beginnings for the Chorale *Ein' Feste Burg;* the student should complete them. (Change of texture is appropriate after a fermata, or after a double bar.) After studying later chapters, this chorale should be scored for full orchestra. The study of Mendelssohn's *Reformation* Symphony—founded on this chorale—should complement the task.

EXAMPLE 15

Ein' Feste Burg: Two Beginnings

(In the second model, it is well to add a stand of cellos to the Bass part.)

CHAPTER IV

Woodwind - Intimate Voices

The woods comprise three distinct types: reedless, single reed, and double reed. Outnumbered greatly by the strings and outweighed in volume by the brass, these small, intimate voices pose formidable problems of balance. Here are the ranges and common territory of the principal instruments:

EXAMPLE 16

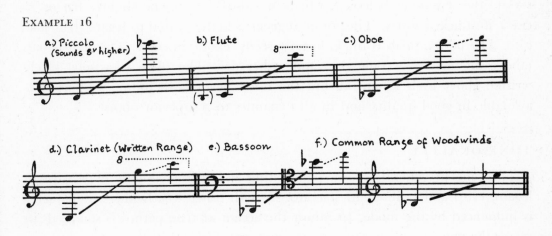

The total range is six octaves (seven if the double bassoon is included); a common range of an eleventh is available. Registers and regions of finest expressive scope are given in the materials on each instrument. The woodwinds are true lyric voices; their foremost and finest rôle is one of expression.

DOUBLE REEDS: THE OBOE

The double reeds present a large group-color, ranging from the soprano (oboe) through the alto (English horn), bass-baritone (bassoon), and profound bass of the double bassoon. Here is a family, nearly related in timbre, strongly

33

unified in character, embracing most of the total wind range. Harmonically and lyrically, double reeds mix with pure and refined effect. Their sound, slightly nasal, is finely expressive.

Like its larger companions, the oboe is conical in shape and overblows at the octave; its fundamental scale extends chromatically from low B-flat to C-sharp on the staff. Its compass and expressive range:

EXAMPLE 17

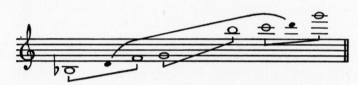

(Brackets indicate registers; arc shows finest solo range.)

The lowest C-sharp tends toward flatness and should not be featured, nor should the semitones below it, which are also likely to be slightly flat or to crack if attacked softly. The lower register is better suited to legato than staccato. The bottom fifth is thick, heavily reedy, exotic in color. The acute notes (above highest D) become thin and rather dry. The oboe is—wisely—rarely written above high E-natural, but the notes beyond, including G-sharp, are available in good quality and in all dynamics to a superior oboist.

TONE QUALITY

The tone in general is tart, penetrating and refined, highly expressive in legato, crisp and pointed in staccato. As with other woodwinds its character is influenced by the mode. In minor the accent of true pathos is sounded, in major the oboe's voice is naïve, rustic, and gay, with a bitter-sweet undertone.

Double and triple tonguing are considered outside the normal means of the oboe, but its capacity for rapid utterance, especially for repeated notes staccato, is considerable. (Do not exceed sixteenth notes in an Allegretto.) It is well known that the oboe requires very little breath. Rests are essential to enable the player to expel unused air!

The oboe is essentially a lyric instrument: its fine-spun tone lends a sensitive, faintly pulsating thread to the musical fabric. Superlative is the held tone (pedal), which delicately supports surrounding strands (see page 37, *Hebrides* Overture of Mendelssohn). The instrument has also unique possibilities of caricature, irony, and the grotesque. Note the wonderful touch in the "Inn Scene" from *Boris:*

EXAMPLE 18

Moussorgsky: *Boris Godounov (Inn Scene)*

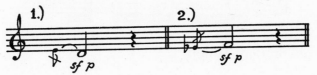

1) Rimsky-Korsakoff version.   2) Original version.

(With this simple means the instrument depicts the wine-bibbing monk and his growing inebriation!)

The finest oboe solos lie in the middle register; they are small in span and often develop tiny tone cells. Witness the *Andante* from Tchaikovsky's Fourth Symphony, the well-known solos in Strauss's *Don Juan* and *Don Quixote,* and the Interlude before Act IV of *Carmen* which is shown here:

EXAMPLE 19

Bizet, *Carmen,* Interlude before Act IV

As a harmonic element, the individualistic oboe tone separates slightly from the smoother colors of flute and clarinet; but in general this presents no serious problem. The blend, however, is better with clarinet.

Arpeggios are too highly characterized to afford a frequent resource. Trills are mainly used in medium register. The tremolo is rare. (See list below of unfavorable trills and tremolos.)

The oboe's sound consorts imperfectly with most strings as unison doubling, although fine examples are not lacking. (The creamy tone of the English horn blends better.) One should remember that the rich, incisive sound—beautiful in limited amounts—tends towards monotony. Hence, the oboe is less used than other woodwinds: one-third to one-half of total playing time of a score is a likely ratio.

As the oboe overblows at the octave, passages which lie on both sides of the break are uneven in tone color:

EXAMPLE 20

Trills (difficult or impossible):

EXAMPLE 21

Tremolos (difficult):

EXAMPLE 22

The above applies to English horn, sounding a perfect fifth lower.

The keys of B, D-flat, and F-sharp are apt to present difficulties.

THE ENGLISH HORN

This is, in effect, an alto oboe in F, extending to concert E-natural below the smaller instrument, and written a *perfect fifth* above pitch. It is cousin, rather than brother, to the oboe. Its tone, melancholy, meditative, and nostalgic, brings a brooding shade to the wind palette. The instrument is the viola of the wood choir.

Within its small mood-compass the English horn is matchless; as Berlioz finely suggests, the instrument conjures up feelings of regret. The tone is grave and noble.

Occasionally its voice, faintly throbbing, borrows the accent of passion, as at the famous union with violas in Tchaikovsky's *Romeo and Juliet*. Another romantic example, stately and eloquent, is its rôle of protagonist in Sibelius's *Swan of Tuonela*.

Wagner's scores provide a veritable dictionary of woodwind combinations: see the use of English horn in *Lohengrin*. Most famous of all solos for this instrument is the "Shepherd's Melody" from Act III of *Tristan*.

The English horn's low octave has a unique quality—full, reedy, and somber, like the hue of a rich madder. Placed in unison with bassoon, horn, or viola, the sound is vibrant and exotic.

While Ravel uses the high (written) E-flat, above the staff, it is well not to exceed the C-natural. This register is strange; it is often doubled with oboe.

The English horn—usually gloomy—shares some of the oboe's talent for biting characterization: parody, sardonic humor, sarcasm. See the "Critic's Section" from Strauss's *Ein Heldenleben;* also, the languorous subject quoted in the Appendix (*Nuages* of Debussy), nostalgic in mood.

THE BASSOON

So consistently valuable is the bassoon that one must consciously ban its over-use. The notes above high B-flat are better avoided, being relatively weak and tending to disturb the embouchure. The bass and tenor clefs are employed; never the treble.

Range, registers, and solo scope:

EXAMPLE 23

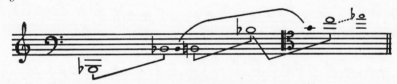

The bassoon's voice is full, throaty, and tense. The fundamental scale extends from deep B-flat up to F on the bass staff. Its lowest octave is heavy and funereal, resembling organ tone; the middle range is warm, reedy, baritone-like, while the top notes are pale or anxious in suggestion. There is something of weariness and disillusion in this register. The highest fifth lacks body and may be readily covered by surrounding tone colors.

The dense low notes are capable of supporting soft brass with ease; the lowest B-flat can be produced with fine *piano* quality. Deep trills and tremolos should be avoided. (See list given later.) Accompaniment formulas are excellent, although strongly characterized. The bassoon *suggests* a certain clumsiness, but this is more apparent than real; the instrument moves with surprising nimbleness. Tonguing technique is similar to that of the oboe, although the bassoon is less lithe, versatile, and precise.

The bassoon is the pessimist of the orchestra. Its tone color is of sallow tinge, its mood often introspective. It is, however, admirably fitted to solemn and mock-solemn pronouncements, and is often called upon to play the "heavy comic." No other instrument so vividly portrays the helplessly ineffectual, the well-intentioned gone awry.

Like the oboe, the bassoon can suggest the sardonic. Its reedy staccato is often invoked for prankish diversions, and while these somewhat sinister buffooneries have been overplayed, they still succeed. The tone of mock diablerie is perfectly sounded in the famous allegro subject of Dukas's *Sorcerer's Apprentice.* For an instance of the high register (somewhat risky), see the opening solo of Stravinsky's *Le Sacre du Printemps,* or the following example from Rimsky-Korsakoff's *Scheherazade:*

EXAMPLE 24

Rimsky-Korsakoff: *Scheherazade* (page 49)

This passage is taxing because of its height and key. (Flat keys are easier than sharp for the bassoon.)

The high bassoon tessitura used in Ravel's *Bolero* forms another difficult specimen.

A superb example of the deepest register occurs at the start of Tchaikovsky's *Pathétique* Symphony. These dense tones have the hue of despair.

SLURS AND TONGUING

Upward slurs are more favorable than downward; in the latter case a "break" may occur. A difficult passage, in this respect, is the subject of the *Valse* from Tchaikovsky's Fifth Symphony.

The lower notes are difficult to attack. They are also taxing for rapid tonguing or for *piano* tonguing.

Some players can accomplish double tonguing, although it is not part of the standard technique. The speed of single tonguing compares with that of the oboe. In general, very rapidly tongued notes lack something of clarity.

As suggested above, lengthy passages in the highest register make excessive demands.

MIXTURES

The bassoon mixes smoothly with all instruments within its pitch range; it blends with the woods as a whole and with brass, notably horns. Its mixture with the three deeper strings is a fine and useful one. Very fine is the unison with violas (see opening of Tchaikovsky's *Marche Slav*). Joined with other reeds, the result is strangely exotic, as in the passage just before *Otello's* death in Verdi's opera—unison of bassoon, clarinet, and English horn.

The instrument's versatility is both a virtue and a failing. Do not abuse it.

TRILLS AND TREMOLOS

The following are difficult or impossible:

EXAMPLE 25

Note that trills on F-sharp (or G-flat) are hazardous in all registers. Above high F-sharp, avoid trills.

Tremolos: use only thirds from low A on bass staff to C a tenth higher.

The lengthy solo in the "Jabberwocky" of Deems Taylor's *Looking Glass* Suite makes excessive demands, covering as it does three octaves and including difficult low trills.

THE DOUBLE BASSOON

This ponderous instrument is related to the bassoon as is the string bass to the cello. Its turgid tones are too massive and intractable for frequent use. As a foundation sound its grave timbre is incomparable when a rich reedy depth is wanted.

While only the two lower octaves are in general use, the tones below bottom D may well be avoided. A certain elephantine humor is within the scope of the instrument; but for solos, the lurching nature of the deep tones carries a degree of danger. Their rumble has a cavernous gloom.

For certain characterizations the instrument is unsurpassed. Listen to the "Beauty and the Beast" episode from Ravel's *Mother Goose:* the beast's mock menace, its good intentions tragically distorted, is wonderfully portrayed by the double bassoon. And see the "Jabberwocky" already mentioned.

The instrument provides a splendid deep foundation in soft, choralelike passages (as Brahms knew),[1] where it powerfully complements the wind choir.

The double bassoon is always written an octave above actual pitch. Only the bass clef is needed. The top octave is of little use.

In general, the double-reed group is the least mobile of the woodwinds and is the most restricted in mood and technical fertility. The instruments may be muted by inserting a handkerchief in the bell. This is a middle-register device. It has not been applied to the bassoon family. Muting is virtually unknown as a woodwind device;[2] it is never applied to the clarinet, whose tone can be reduced to vanishing point without artificial aid.

THE CLARINET

This is a single reed, mainly cylindrical in bore, overblowing at the twelfth. Details of its (written) range:

EXAMPLE 26

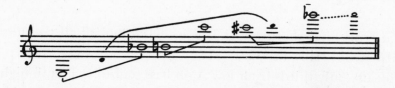

Ductility is the mark of the clarinet; in technical address it competes with the flute and the violin. The spacious range offers vivid contrasts. The *chalumeau* (lowest) octave is spectral and hollow, painting in the darkest shades.

---

[1] For a fine example, see the *Adagio, più andante* (last movement) of Brahms's First Symphony.
[2] Stravinsky uses three oboes, muted, at the close of *Petrouchka*.

The "throat" register (written G to B on the staff) is technically treacherous: it is hazy in color, ideal for touching in faint grays. The "break" occurs at the point of overblowing, at middle B (written note). As the medium and upper ranges are reached, the tone becomes purer and more clarionlike (whence the name clarinet).

Berlioz has called the clarinet an epic instrument; but its note is one of passion and poetry rather than of heroism. Its accent is exquisitely turned, its tone of silken smoothness.

DYNAMIC VIRTUES

The instrument is supremely endowed in dynamic values. No other wind approaches its ultra-*piano*. Wonderfully pliable, the clarinet copes easily with virtually all technical problems. Scales and arpeggios of gauzy lightness; legato and staccato patterns (including a beautifully articulated half-staccato); wide skips up or down; elaborate embroideries, repeated notes, trills and tremolos —all are within its familiar duties. Single-tonguing is normal, though some players have mastered double-tongue technique.

TWO MAIN VARIETIES

The clarinet is a transposing instrument. The clarinet in C is obsolete; today the principal clarinets are built in B-flat and A. Most players favor the B-flat instrument as being more brilliant and accurate in intonation. Often the larger instrument (in A) is used for sharp keys. If the low concert C-sharp is required, it is advisable to use the A-clarinet; the latter's color is slightly darker and fuller, especially in the lowest octave. (Few can distinguish between the clarinets in B-flat and A.) But above the staff the instrument in A tends to be slightly sharp.

Passages which *feature* the throat register or break are problematical. Fingering problems and tonal neutrality characterize this region. However, figures which merely traverse this area offer few difficulties. The sensitive notes are G-sharp, A, and B-flat on the staff. The color here is very quiet.

Beginning with B just above the break, the clarinet can produce a true glissando. Below this—in the fundamental range—a fake glissando (chromatic scale) is used. The beginning of the *Rhapsody in Blue* is a well-known model. Flutter-tongue is possible, although doubtful, mainly because players have not cultivated this technique.

CONTRIBUTIONS OF WEBER

Among the first to penetrate the expressive-dramatic possibilities of the clarinet was Weber. Famous pioneer examples of the *chalumeau* notes are found near the opening of the *Freischütz* Overture; later in this score occurs an equally renowned instance of the medium and throat registers. (In considering Weber's gift of tonal depiction, it is significant to note that he was trained in his youth in painting.)

Since the instrument overblows mainly at the twelfth, octave alternations are less congenial than is the case with the other woods. They should not be written in rapid tempo.

The speed of tonguing should not exceed sixteenths at 124 to the quarter note.

Accompaniment figures, such as arpeggios, have an oily glibness which has been much exploited. Their effect, unless extremely soft, verges on banality. But for the proper situation, the ghostlike *pianissimo* of these broken chords has a unique quality. Their gentle sound in the low and middle registers is like the softest spray of tone.

The soft pedal has been employed with poetic effect. It beautifully suggests the line of a distant horizon.

THE SUBTONE

An unusual method of production is the so-called subtone, used in the *chalumeau* register. The player touches the side of the reed lightly with his tongue. The sound is ultra-soft: faintly perceptible. It is almost exclusively a microphone procedure. We know of no example of its use in the standard literature.

Slurring is easy for a good player. Upward slurs are less difficult; wide slurs which traverse the break show a change of color. Before a wide skip it is well to insert a brief rest.

The B-flat clarinet is written a major second above actual pitch; that in A, a minor third higher than it sounds. The treble clef is always used.

Alone among woodwind players, symphony clarinetists have virtually eschewed the use of vibrato. The result has been a cool, objective tone quality, admirable in certain instances, deprived of glowing warmth in others. The point of view seems to be slowly changing, perhaps because of the style of a few celebrated exponents of the instrument, which makes fastidious use of the vibrato resource.

TRILLS AND TREMOLOS

These trills present problems:

EXAMPLE 27

Tremolos are possible almost to the octave if the top note does not exceed C above the staff. Avoid:

EXAMPLE 28

Tremolos involving the following as upper notes are poor:

EXAMPLE 29

Avoid octave leaps from low to medium register:

EXAMPLE 30

THE SMALL CLARINETS

It is unfortunate that the smaller clarinets, which include those in D and in E-flat, are so infrequently used in the orchestra. Their clear, biting tone is invaluable for certain characterizations (see *Finale* of Berlioz's *Fantastic Symphony* and Strauss's *Till Eulenspiegel*). Wonderfully effective for incisive portraiture—and parody—are these instruments. Their tone substitutes a steely brilliance for the caressing warmth of the ordinary instruments.

THE BASS CLARINET

Built in B-flat, the bass clarinet is the octave brother of the regular clarinet. It should be written in treble clef, a major ninth above sound, although German musicians often write a major second above, using bass clef.

No other deep wind can approach the bass clarinet's full and velvety *piano*. Its value is great in the total wind scheme, and it shares the technical resources of the smaller clarinet, though on a more limited scale. (Large instruments cannot "speak" as fluently as the smaller types.) The tone is on the gloomy side: vague, windy, and unhappy. The lowest octave is darkly shaded and effective for somber colorings, shadowy brush strokes, suggestions of mystery or surprise. See Tchaikovsky's *Nutcracker* Suite, "Dance of the Sugar Plum Fairy." Only the bottom two octaves are commonly used, the upper notes being superior on ordinary clarinet.

Beautiful in color is the mixture of bass clarinet and soft horns or trombones; and strange is its combination with deep percussion. Low trills have a curious windy color unlike any other orchestral sound.

The family of saxophones is discussed in Chapter XII, among the jazz-band techniques.

THE FLUTE

The flute's range embraces a clear three octaves, starting at middle C (some flutes possess an extra semitone below):

EXAMPLE 31

Its fundamental scale extends to C-sharp on the staff, the upper octaves being obtained by overblowing: altering the pressure of the air stream, and slightly varying the angle. The notes of the basic scale can also be overblown at the twelfth; their quality is slightly thinner, and their use is rare. They are indicated by a small circle over the sounding note.

Formerly made of wood, the flute is now usually built of silver, platinum, or gold. Its timbre, or coloration, varies slightly according to the substance. Metal flutes are considered more brilliant than the earlier wood variety.[3]

Gevaert, speaking of the flute, acutely remarks:

By its method of tone production, as well as by its pitch, it forms a contrast to the human voice (our larynx is a reed instrument), and for that reason the flute is unable to give expression to the stirring cry of passion; its ethereal breath lacks warmth and life.

And perhaps because of its aloofness, the flute has a serene, almost timeless quality. Its images, mirrorlike, are at once faithful and unreal. It observes rather than takes part in the human scene. Yet, while its nature is reflective and detached, it can speak with emotion. (See the celebrated Gluck extract mentioned below.)

The lowest octave of the flute is dark, sultry, curiously trumpetlike; the notes *seem* to sound out-of-tune. These breathy sounds suggest the soft contralto voice. Rapid figures in this area are less clear than the higher tones; the speed of emission is reduced by about eight degrees on the metronome. This register is easily obscured and must be delicately accompanied. Often two or three flutes are used for a deep unison. (See the haunting passage in the middle movement of Debussy's *Ibéria*.)

The middle octave is bland and silken, slightly thick, and beautifully expressive. The end of Act II of *Die Meistersinger* is a fine example of lower-middle register; still more famous is the matchless solo which opens the *Afternoon of a Faun*. And, what is perhaps the most beautiful of all flute melodies, the Elysian Fields scene from Gluck's *Orfeo*.

THE HIGHEST OCTAVE

Strauss points out the contemporary preference for the highest octave,[4] remarking that in this register the tone separates from, instead of blending with, the ensemble, thus losing some of its enriching effect. Nonetheless, the top octave is of the greatest value: the tint—silvery, pure, and frosty—is unique. Its exhilarating color adds gleaming lights to the ensemble, while its clear, whistling timbre is ideally adapted to certain moods. The Interlude to Act III of *Carmen* calls for the top B-flat in *piano*.

In this register the flute is wonderfully transparent; at soft dynamic shades it seems to impart cool reflections and to clarify the harmonics of other woods.

[3] The view is firmly held by some acousticians that the material of the instrument does not affect its tone quality; the determining factors being the shape and proportions of the air column and the mouthpiece or embouchure. Theory and fact seem to disagree here.

[4] In his elaborate revision of Berlioz's *Instrumentation:* see Bibliography.

Here is a unique example—the *"Sous Bois"* from Chabrier's *Suite Pastorale* —of crossing registers. Note the fine echo effect of the clarinet at bar 5 (large score) and the delicate silver-filigree touches of the flute at the last bar: it adds tiny accents to the violin line—

EXAMPLE 32

Chabrier: opening of *"Sous Bois"* from *Suite Pastorale* (large score)

TECHNICAL POWERS

Technically, nearly all things are possible. Exceeding the clarinet in mobility, the flute is master of every device. Patterns based on repeated notes (single, double, and triple tonguing) are highly characteristic. All decorations—trills, turns, tremolos, scales, appoggiaturas, figurations—are at its command. Scales, diatonic and chromatic, are admirably smooth, and emerge crisply in staccato, especially in the medium and high octaves. Legato is pure and refined.

The two highest semitones (B and C) should not be written *piano*. (Strauss confesses to this error.) Octave skips are easy and excellent. The high register is slightly more difficult, owing to finger and embouchure problems. Rapid alternation of notes between high and medium registers also presents some difficulty.

The trills above highest G are better not written *piano;* trills on high B and C and on the lowest C and C-sharp are impractical. The flutter-tongue is relatively easy. Its effect is curious and charming at soft dynamics (see Strauss's *Don Quixote* quoted in Appendix); in *forte* the sound is rough and buzzing. Wide skips are favorable for the most part. Flat keys are preferred by the flute.

Here are some hazardous trills and tremolos:

EXAMPLE 33

Confine tremolos to minor third except on:

EXAMPLE 34

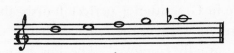

Starting on the above notes, tremolos may be written up to perfect fourths. Octave alternations are good.

For an especially difficult flute passage, see the last page of the *Sorcerer's Apprentice*.

We have successfully experimented with muting the flute by directing the player to insert a piece of soft tissue in the tube after removing the foot-joint. The musical passage was situated in the medium-high register.

THE PICCOLO

This miniature flute (sometimes called *ottavino*) is always written an octave below its sounding pitch. Its practical range is slightly narrower than that of the flute—from low D to high B-flat.

Whereas the earlier use of the piccolo was confined usually to situations of climax or program painting (especially "storm" scenes), modern feeling has assigned the instrument a wider rôle. The low and medium registers have a peculiar expressive possibility; their wan and disembodied timbre is unique among the tone colors. For these ranges, a light background is necessary.

The piccolo gains in penetrative force as it enters the top octave. Here its tone has a flashing edge which survives in the fiercest tutti. These high sounds flicker like sparks above the tonal landscape. They are sometimes used (with fine effect) to suggest tiny bells. They have, too, a curious mechanical, twittering character, which is emphasized by their distance from the human voice-range.[5]

Generally the piccolo is used as octave companion of the flute, sometimes two octaves above clarinet (see third Interlude, *Carmen*), oboe, or even bassoon.

It mixes delightfully with all bright colors: high harp, pizzicato, glockenspiel, triangle, xylophone: its thin note is like fine gilding.

The piccolo's technique is a counterpart of that of the flute; the second or third flutist doubles on the small instrument. The table of trills and tremolos given for the flute applies, sounding an octave higher.

THE ALTO FLUTE

This beautiful flute in G, written a perfect fourth above its sound, is unfortunately rather rare. As written, the range is that of the flute, but only the two lower octaves are usually employed. The low notes require a good deal

---

[5] Rimsky-Korsakoff, in his *Principles of Orchestration,* points out the curious impression imparted by instruments whose usual range is remote from those of human voices.

of breath; in this region rests are desirable. The same holds good for the ordinary flute.

The tone is full, velvety, warm, but somewhat easily covered. Ravel (in his *Daphnis et Chloé*) and Stravinsky (in *Le Sacre du Printemps*) are among modern composers who have made fine use of this instrument. Rimsky-Korsakoff uses the alto flute in *Mlada, Christmas Night, Sadko,* and in other of his later operas.

THE WOODWIND ENSEMBLE

The effective combination of the woods depends on an intimate understanding of their idiosyncrasies. Particularly important is the character of the registers of each family. Thus, the double reeds are strong and thick in the low register, superior in the middle region, thin and less expressive in the acute area. The flute is rich, but somewhat weak, in the bottom octave; its strongest region lies above the staff. The lowest octave of the clarinets is cloudy and somber; the throat register is weak, while the upper half of its range becomes clear and penetrating. These factors are of cardinal importance for the successful combination of the four instruments, notably in chord constructions. Here is a D major chord scored in several ways:

EXAMPLE 35

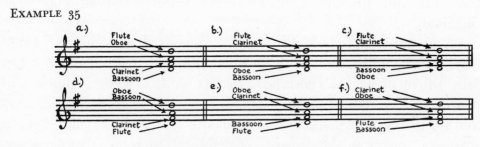

    a. Clarinet lacks color; D-reeds conspicuous.
    b. Oboe conspicuous.
    c. D-reeds conspicuous.
    d. Flute and clarinet weak; D-reeds conspicuous.
    e. Flute weak; bassoon conspicuous.
    f. D-reeds conspicuous.

Generally speaking, a medium or low chord in close position with different instruments on each particle will be unsatisfactory, although a high chord will be more successful.

PART WRITING

Fine part writing is imperative where tone colors of distinct character are present. The ear perceives clearly the conduct of each line; blemishes and departures from the normal are easily detected. Unusual procedures (such as oboe above flute, clarinet below bassoon) are sometimes effective but should be based on *expression* instead of novelty. Idiomatic writing for each type, distinction of rhythm, artistic phrasing and dynamics are essential to good results.

Double reeds mix excellently in two-, three-, or four-part writing. The same holds true for mixtures of flutes and clarinets. The single reeds mix well with all families, although the *chalumeau* area is apt to be conspicuous. That octave, however, produces a fine, dark, exotic color in mixture with bassoon. Memorable also is the union of low English horn and clarinet; if the oboe is added, the reedy quality is intensified, and the tone becomes richly pungent.

DOUBLINGS AND BALANCE

Unison doublings depend for their effect upon the registers used. Given players of equal ability, an even balance results when both instruments are in similar registers. When different registers are in play, for unison doubling, the instrument set in an extreme register—high or low—will be likely to predominate. The same principle holds for octave doubling and for doubling at other intervals.

Passages in thirds and sixths between instruments of the same type sound excellent; fourths, fifths, and all dissonant doublings show intensified color, especially where oboes are concerned. In fact, it is a modern practice to heighten dissonance by this means.

Reverting to the octave spacing, instruments of the same color have a piquant sound, owing to the disparity of register. Two-octave doublings further accentuate this opposition of color.

An exquisite example of the diminished octave relation (not a doubling) is found (in bar 5) in the "Carillon" from the first *Arlésienne Suite*. This is illustrated in Example 36. Observe the utter simplicity of the string background.

EXAMPLE 36

Bizet: *L'Arlésienne* Suite, No. 1 (page 48)

Here the clash of color and register of the two flutes—each tracing its own pattern—has a delicious effect.

IMPORTANCE OF RESTS

The inclusion of rests takes on added importance when wind instruments are employed. Aside from their artistic contribution, they provide relief for the performer. A tired player is a mediocre player. Rests, well placed, help the breathing problem and contribute to clear phrasing.

Monotony can be avoided by utilizing the large range of the instruments (averaging some three octaves). Avoid the tame effect which results from over-use of the middle register. The latter is a common error.

As mentioned before, the oboe is apt to play a smaller part in the scheme than the other woodwinds. The bottom register of the bassoon is often over-used, although the latter may be effectively separated by an octave or more from the other instruments. The choice of registers for chord building is extremely important; it spells the difference between good and bad balance. Musical invention must spring from the instrument itself—its natural idiom. Symphonic literature is rich in such models; these should be carefully studied. Finally, every detail—accent, articulation, phrasing, dynamic—must be scrupulously set down.

Effects of beauty and distinction can result from sensitive part writing. Few musical thoughts possess greater charm than the simple dialogue of two woodwinds. In such passages the instruments may cross freely.

HARMONIC PRINCIPLES

Three procedures are used in harmonic writing: 1. Overlaying; 2. Interlocking; 3. Enclosure:

EXAMPLE 37

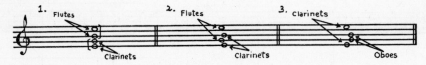

In the first, the color of each member group retains much of its identity. The second method (most widely used) results in fused tone color; enclosure, the rarest procedure, is generally used for an octave pedal framing inner moving parts. Practice and study examples of each method.

Note that close position sounds well (in all dynamics) between instruments of the same or related timbres. Open writing is transparent and produces dispersion of color. Use of extreme registers should be reserved for special effects demanding intensified hues.

Further discussion of part writing, harmonic, and coloristic principles will be found in Chapters IX and X.

EXERCISES

Invent solo passages for each woodwind, exploiting the several registers, tonguings, and technical idioms. Place rests carefully. Every detail counts.

Write counterpoints in two or more parts, considering relations of registers. Phrase carefully and sensitively.

Arrange triad forms, using three or more woodwinds, up to ten, for the solution of sonorities and balance problems. The same for seventh chords in open and close positions. (For all inversions except the second, the bass tone is usually undoubled in the upper parts. Doubling of the dissonant particle produces voice-leading problems; when used it needs careful handling.)

Score for woodwinds Nos. 4, 7, 9, 26, of Schumann's *Album for the Young;* Scarlatti, Sonata No. 11. (Kalmus Edition). Score the same examples for woods plus strings.

CHAPTER V

Heroic Expression: The Brass

Admirably compact and sonorous, the brass instruments add an invaluable resource of color, power, and balanced sonority. Their sound is manly, their expression forthright. Bold affirmation, the heroic, the knightly, and the martial—these moods they communicate with commanding force.

We divide the brasses into two closely related groups: the horn (French horn) and tuba—expansive, dark in color—and the bright trumpet-trombone segment, capable of more incisive and animated suggestion. Here are the ranges, registers, and fields of best expression:

EXAMPLE 38

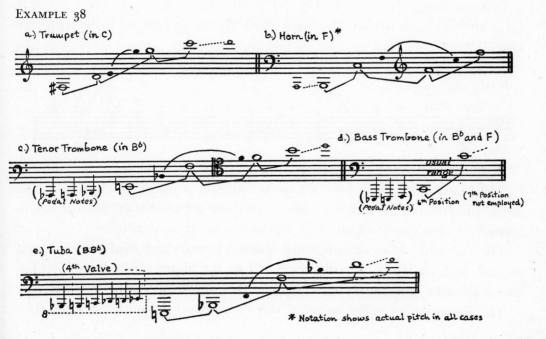

THE HORN

The brass group is less versatile than the string and wood choirs. Its sound is heavier, its emission less fluid, and while the harmonic potential is of immense value, the choir contributes far less as a lyric resource. But a general exception is provided by the horn. Its warm, noble tone lends itself well to the poetic and meditative: its sound is clothed in the colors of romance. Yet the horn has a dual nature; upon command it can be defiant, assertive, dramatic, and vital.

The magical notes that sound from Oberon's horn call up a haunting view of fairyland (opening of the *Oberon* Overture):

EXAMPLE 39

Weber: Overture to *Oberon* (opening bar)

Three notes! With these Weber has made a mood of enchantment.

In considering the brass family, we must memorize the overtone series as far as the sixteenth partial (the black notes are not in tune with the tempered system):

EXAMPLE 40

The brass technique is founded upon this tone series, of which number one is the fundamental. Horns are able to produce all sixteen except the fundamental (though rarely required to use the two or three highest).

The "natural" brass—in use until about a century ago—had a fixed fundamental, and was thus virtually restricted to the above limited group. (The use of "crooks" and "stopping" enlarged this primitive scheme.)

The invention of valves enabled the instruments instantly to alter their length of tubing, and from a new fundamental to draw upon a shifted series.[1] Although the natural horns and trumpets have now vanished from the orchestra, it is true that their tradition and idiom survive to some extent in the present instruments. Fine brass writing often displays, as a vestigial influence, the scheme of the overtone series. At the same time we can frankly accept the fact that the brasses are now chromatic instruments and can banish certain inhibitions based on classic writing.

For simple models of horn writing based on the natural overtones, see the *Finale* of Beethoven's Fifth Symphony and the opening of Brahms's Symphony No. 2.

THE PRESENT-DAY HORN

Today most symphony players use a "double horn"; that is, one that is pitched in F but equipped with a thumb valve which throws the instrument into B-flat, a fourth above. The reason is as simple as it is important. Glancing again at the harmonic series, the reader will note that the intervals become steadily smaller as the series mounts. From the seventh partial upward, there is a scalelike series. The player produces the partials by means of lip tension and air pressure—*embouchure*. The production of the higher partials takes a most delicate adjustment of embouchure, since the partials are so closely compressed. From the shorter B-flat tubing the player is able to sound the *same pitches as lower numbers* in the harmonic series. This is a matter of vital importance, since the medium partials are easier and safer to produce.

The horn's reputation as an unpredictable and hazardous instrument rests largely upon the treacherous character of the upper partials. In any case, the student is well advised to approach the higher notes *by step or easy skip,* and to make scant use of the written notes above the staff, especially in soft dynamic shades.

NOTATION

The horn in F (the part is written in F in all cases) is notated a *perfect* fifth above actual sound; when the bass clef is used, it is the general custom to write a fourth below pitch. The latter custom has nothing to commend it;

[1] The first valve lowers the pitch one tone; the second valve, a half tone; the third, a tone and a half.

adopt a uniform notation for treble and bass clefs, with a footnote in the part to advise the player as to bass-clef transposition.

Horn parts influenced by vocal tradition, or triadic in nature, are likely to be practical. A part that the player can conceive mentally will "come off" well; on the contrary, writing that is thick with eccentric skips will always be more hazardous. The straightforward, the clear and flowing, usually proves successful. It is unwise to *attack* written notes above the staff as solo; remember that the player's task constantly involves delicate mental and physical adjustments. Also, remember that these high partials are more difficult to produce in *piano*. Tones *sounding* below the bass staff should not be featured or placed in an exposed situation. They should move deliberately.

SAFETY IN NUMBERS

The adage, "safety in numbers" (or "misery loves company!") ever holds in the case of this instrument. A few horns in unison will generally perform with greater dash and confidence than a single player. But there is no substitute for the beautifully subjective effect of solo playing.

GROUPING OF HORNS

The modern orchestra includes four horn parts (a fifth player sometimes relieves the first hornist). The quartet is divided in two groups: Horns one and three play the higher strands; the others cultivate a style suited to lower-note production.

The lowest octave of the horn (the total range is three and a half octaves) is capable of little in the way of mobility. Simple parts, such as pedals or sedate stepwise movement, with provision for frequent rest, form the best writing. The low notes have less power; however, they possess a fine velvety quality and mix well with the other deep instruments, especially in the softer dynamics. Essentially the horn is a middle-register instrument.

MUTES AND MUTING

The player can mute the instrument by moving his right hand further into the bell, or by inserting a mute. He prefers the latter method, which produces a more distinct tone. Metal mutes raise the pitch a half step; fiber mutes do not alter the pitch. The latter variety gives a softer, more distant sound. For harsh, tangy effects write a cross over the note and the indication "Brassy" or "*Cuivré*." The result is piercing and acidlike.

Mutes are generally ineffective in the lowest register; these notes are difficult to attack, while accurate intonation is unlikely.[2] Muting the highest notes of the horn produces a curious quality; they are less commonly used. (See Appendix, Ex. 2.) After a muted passage the indication "Open" (or *Senza*) should be written.

Strauss, who has provided so many magnificent models of horn writing, is not always the best master to imitate. The superbly vital motive for four united horns from *Don Juan* reveals the instruments at their heroic best:

EXAMPLE 41

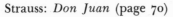

Strauss: *Don Juan* (page 70)

On the other hand, owing to its great range, the famous solo at the opening of *Till Eulenspiegel* is an example of virtuoso style that is better avoided by a less gifted personality. (Avoid sudden, wide skips, unless the interval is an octave.)

A few well-known examples by other masters: the sensitive solo passage in the slow movement of Tchaikovsky's Fifth Symphony; the luminous openings of Schubert's C major Symphony and Brahms's B-flat Piano Concerto; the exquisite folklike phrase in the final scene of Stravinsky's *Fire Bird;* the quartet of horns near the opening of the *Freischütz* Overture; the phantomlike stopped horns at the close of *Pétrouchka*. The nineteenth century—the Romantic hundred-years—abounds in fine examples of horn writing.

TONGUING

The horn is able to accomplish all varieties of tonguing. While its emission is less crisp than that of the trumpets (the horn is somewhat on the languid side), repeated rhythms at rapid speed fare excellently. The latter should,

---

[2] But see the low concert F-sharps in the *Finale* of the *Pathétique* Symphony of Tchaikovsky. The ghostly passage for a quartet of soft-muted horns at the close of *Pétrouchka* is a beautiful contemporary example.

however, be placed in the medium or medium-high register and should not be protracted. To surmount the fatigue problem, the horns may relieve each other in lengthy, tongued passages. Here, to divide is to conquer. (The same device is used for all wind instruments.)

The pedal is a frequent and excellent effect, used either as single note or as octave. Horn octaves are in general of fine character (see the opening of Tchaikovsky's Fourth Symphony). Trills are best placed in the medium-high register. They are produced with the valves and are brilliantly penetrating in *forte,* especially during a crescendo.

The horn produces an effect of glissando by sounding rapidly (upward) a segment of the overtone series, using its higher register:

EXAMPLE 42

The transposition of horns is invariably downward, in relation to the note C. Thus, horns in E transpose a minor sixth down; those in B-flat alto, a major second; in B-flat basso, a major ninth, and so forth. But, as noted above, the F horn is standard at the present time.

THE TRUMPET

This is the soprano of the brass choir, the most fluent and technically gifted, barring the cornet. Tunes of a bracing, open-air nature suit it well; while sentimental ideas take on a maudlin tinge. The trumpet is manly and direct —its brilliant color calls up scenes of chivalry. The middle register affords the finest solo region. From low E to high G the instrument is at its best, commanding the whole dynamic range (although a true *pianissimo* calls for a gifted trumpeter). The deep notes (below the staff, especially beneath low C) are somewhat thick and bulky—slightly gross. Here the crisp and crackling tonguing for which the instrument is famous is less incisive.

The trumpet's ringing tone is immensely effective as reinforcement in tutti; its glittering color pierces the massed ensemble like a shaft of light. Its note is epic; not by chance did Wagner confide to the trumpet the Sword Motive of his Tetralogy.

Slurs—which in wind instruments are usually easier in an upward direction
—should not exceed an octave, while the major seventh is rather difficult. The
glissando—a half-valve effect—is available, and is effective from low C upward.
(It is rare in symphonic music.) It is better not to exceed an octave in glissando. The *flare* is a short glissando (dance-band device) placed before a strong
attack; it is written:

EXAMPLE 43

Superbly clear and compelling are the three types of tonguing. They are
invariably successful, but, as with the horns, should not be unduly protracted.
In strong dynamics the tongue articulates more slowly. For single tonguing,
do not exceed 126 to a quarter note; double tonguing, 184 to a quarter; triple,
116 to a quarter, in dynamics not above *mezzo forte* (*mf*). Slower speeds must
prevail in the lowest fourth of the range.

Trills are round and firm; the half-tone trills are easier to finger. Avoid trills
below the bottom C-sharp and those on high F, F-sharp, G, and G-sharp.

A simple and interesting device is to begin a trill, in woodwinds or violins,
at the moment that the trumpet attacks a high note. The latter may retain or
release the tone during the trill. Wagner uses this means in *Götterdämmerung*
(p. 432), but places the trill of oboes and clarinets one bar after the trumpet
attacks high G.

MUTES

Symphonic composers generally write *con sordino* without further qualifi-
cation. It is well to realize, what the jazz player has long known, that there
are many trumpet mutes available, each imparting a different shade of color
and volume. The usual (straight) mute is made of metal, plastic, or fiber (the
last-named produces the softest quality). Further, there are the varieties known
as Harmon, Robinson, Stoneline, Solotone, and Whisper.

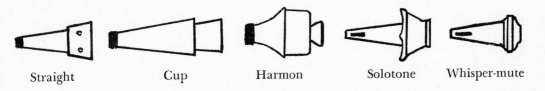

Straight   Cup   Harmon   Solotone   Whisper-mute

Dance-band players produce, with mutes, rapidly tongued effects of incredibly light and liquid character.

Symphony players do not consider these mutes as normal equipment. But time will alter this attitude. The student is urged to become acquainted with the sound and nature of these mutes. The hat mute may also be employed. However, it may possibly lower the pitch.

All mutes convey an effect of distance when used in *piano*. In *forte* their pinched, attenuated timbre adds a quality of intense and pungent power, invaluable for effects of caricature or of the grotesque. The mute's power of portraiture is vividly heard in the "Goldenberg" episode from the *Pictures at an Exhibition,* scored by Ravel.

KEYS OF THE TRUMPET

The trumpet in general use is pitched in B-flat. But the C trumpet is coming into greater use [3] and presents certain advantages in the way of response, intonation, and high range. The B-flat instrument has a fuller tone; its sound has richness and life. It is written a whole tone above actual pitch. While its mobility is slightly less than that of the C instrument, its quality of color compensates in the mind of most players. The worst notes on the B-flat instrument are low C-sharp and D.

The small trumpet (in D, written a whole tone below its sounding pitch) is valuable for extremely high ranges. Its sound, though brilliant, is thin and cutting. Aside from eighteenth-century music, it has been used occasionally in recent scores, especially by Stravinsky (see last page of *Pétrouchka*); unfortunately the instrument is not commonly available.

The large F trumpet, used often by the French composers and by Strauss and Puccini, has been supplanted by the B-flat instrument. The former transposes a perfect fourth *above*.

The bass trumpet has been used by Wagner in the *Nibelungen Ring*. It is pitched an octave lower than the ordinary instrument.

DYNAMICS

Above high G the tone of the trumpet becomes increasingly thin and penetrating. These high notes are unfavorable for the softer dynamics, except for superlative players. In general the extreme notes should be sparingly used.

[3] The Boston Symphony trumpet section employs C trumpets.

They are generally found at moments of musical stress, when they add biting colors to the emotional scheme.

It is difficult to secure a subtle dynamic range with the trumpet. The middle register offers the best area for quiet dynamics.

THE CORNET

This facile instrument, mainly favored by the French School, has by snobbish consent been banished from the American symphonic scene. Finely played, its smooth, warm legato has a persuasive quality, while its phenomenal technical powers approach those of the flute and clarinet. In fact, the cornet is the coloratura of the brass section. It is kin to the horn and tuba in quality. A certain glibness has thrown it into disfavor. No doubt the cornet is docile rather than distinguished. But its quiet, round color can add the softest shades to the brass palette. The instrument, in this country, has been associated with music of paltry character. That is its misfortune.

The cornet's written range is similar to the trumpet's, the best register lying between low C and high G. It is pitched in B-flat.

THE TROMBONE

The symphonic trombone is without valves. Its slide, moving through seven positions, lengthens the tubing by successive semitones. Thus the tenor trombone, pitched in B-flat (first position) descends in the seventh position to E-natural (see table below). The instrument, however, is able to produce its fundamental—known as pedal tone; the first three of these are in common use. The following diagram shows the positions and the upper partials commonly available. (Unlike the horn, the trombone and trumpet rarely employ the partials above number eight; while the trumpet and horn do not in practice utilize their fundamentals.)

EXAMPLE 44

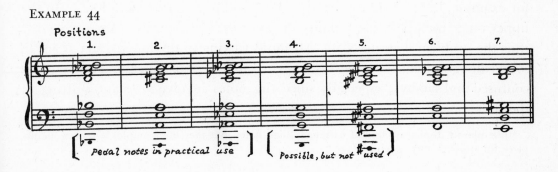

The usual trombone section consists of two tenor and one bass trombone. The bass instrument is sometimes built in B-flat, but has a larger bore and is equipped with a valve device which shifts the fundamental to F, a fourth below. While there are increasing numbers of tenor trombones equipped with this attachment, its use is not as yet standardized.

The trombone's rôle is that of power, dignity, weight, and brilliance. Its tone is at once massive and pure, and despite its primitive slide principle, the instrument commands a subtle legato. (Obviously, all tones lying in a single position can be produced with a natural legato; when the slide has to be employed the performer's art comes subtly into play.)

While it is possible to produce the tones above high B-flat as far as E-flat (as in Schumann's Third Symphony), these notes are difficult technically and dynamically.[4] High B-flat or B-natural is a good practical top limit. Bass and tenor clefs are employed.

The deep notes of the instrument, especially the pedal tones, have a fine solemn quality in *piano*. They take a good deal of breath. The pedal tones demand preparation; precede them with a brief rest. Leaps of more than an octave should be avoided if possible when pitches above high G are involved. All high tones, played *forte,* have great impact.

REGION OF WEAKNESS

The danger spot lies in the diminished fifth:

EXAMPLE 45

Avoid all rapid interchanges of notes demanding a wide shift of position; for example, the notes B-flat and low E, A and low E, B-flat and low F. In the upper range the player has a choice of more than one position for each note: thus the problem does not arise. All rapid writing in the low register is apt to sound disagreeable; here the instrument cannot speak quickly. The result is confused and labored, especially since the notes involve constant shifting of the slide.

---

[4] Jazz players display no fear of extremely high notes, but they often employ a special mouthpiece for trumpet and trombone.

All tonguings are available. Sixteenth notes with the quarter moving at 126 will usually be double or triple tongued, although single tonguing can go at considerable speed. Soft tonguing (using a *du* instead of a *tu* attack) is an important technical feature, and permits faster articulation as well as smooth tone quality. Rapid tonguing should be avoided in the low register except for occasional brief detached patterns.

Remember that the breathing factor is of enormous importance. Avoid long slurs, and relieve the player with well-placed rests; even short rests are of great assistance. This question is of particular importance in the grave register, especially when the dynamic exceeds *mezzo piano*.

MUTES

Only the straight mute is in common use, and this much less often than for the trumpet. Its effect is not too successful. The result is to stifle the instrument; the fine tonal bloom is lost, and the sensation is one of struggle. If the mute is used, allow the player some ten seconds to insert it. Example of its use for three trombones will be found on pages 8 and 9 of Strauss's *Don Quixote*.

In the top octave the trombone's tone is clear and dazzling. High chords, in close position, have a fiery glow. This is the region in which the trombone excels in bold proclamation and vivid color. Open position also carries through with magnificent effect in simple chord forms. Dissonances, played *forte,* have savage power.

United trombones lend immense impact to passages of stern nature. Deliberate movement suits them well; yet the instruments can move with astonishing speed in the upper half of their range. (During the time it took to reach the radio dial, we have heard a good part of the *Flight of the Bumble Bee* warbled by solo trombone!)

Trills are *possible* in the upper register, but are almost never employed in orchestral writing. They are made with the *embouchure* (lip trills).

A characteristic example of solo declamation is the priestlike passage in Rimsky-Korsakoff's *Russian Easter*. Bold passages for the instrument can be found in Elgar's *Enigma* Variations and *Falstaff,* while the scores of Wagner and Berlioz abound in fine examples.

Employ the trombone relatively little; it will then gain in effect. (During the greater part of *Pelléas et Mélisande* the big brass is silent; but what an effect it makes when it is called upon!) On the other hand, its contribution in soft situations can be of great beauty. Here it can take the place of the usually overworked horns for quiet chord forms or soft pedals. Deep fifths and fourths have unique strength and richness.

The instrument has a remarkable dynamic scale, and adds immeasurably to growing sonorities. Even greater than the horns and trumpets is its power of *forte piano (fp)* or of making suddenly swelling or decreasing dynamics. The *glissando,* in all registers, is peculiarly effective.

All the brass is capable of flutter-tongue. The effect is one of painful stridence in the *forte;* coarse and rending in character. In *piano* the device has curious suggestions of uneasiness. (See the example from *Don Quixote* quoted in Appendix.) We repeat the caution respecting the low register: here rapid rhythms and tonguings are hazardous.

THE BASS TUBA

The bass tuba is the Big Bertha of the brass. Built in various sizes and shapes, the status of the tuba is unprecise; there is not space to enumerate the various members of this family. We shall accept as model the instrument in BB-flat, capable of touching the lowest B-flat of the piano, although this pitch is not in normal use. The following practical range is available to a good bass tuba player:

EXAMPLE 46

The tuba, broadly conical in bore, provides a powerful foundation for the wind band. Rich and warm—although gloomy—in tone color, it is more nearly allied to the horn family than to its usual associates, the trombones. Its massive *forte* is exceeded in force only by the percussive instruments. The low tones are thick and somewhat slow of emission. They have a blurting quality; when driven dynamically these sounds display a rending savagery. But despite its size, the tuba is capable of real mobility and can offer a *piano* of fine subdued quality. Its powers of characterization and caricature are great: in *Pétrouchka,* Stravinsky employs the high register adroitly to sketch the lumbering bear (page 115, miniature score):

EXAMPLE 47

Stravinsky: *Pétrouchka* (page 115)

Here the pinched tones afford precisely the uncouth, loutish color required.

The "Bydlo" episode from *Pictures at an Exhibition* (see Appendix) takes the instrument up to extreme high G-sharp. Ravel's practice at this point is definitely not one to be imitated.

Aside from such occasional solo features, the instrument is mainly employed to add substance and color to the bass line (as in the *Meistersinger* Overture, wherein, doubled by bassoon and cello, it has a famous passage terminating with a trill on medium-high A).

HARMONIC FUNCTION

Its harmonic function, as substratum of the brass tutti, is of marked value, although as suggested above it does not form an ideal union with trombones. Rimsky-Korsakoff opposes the standard octave-doubling of bass trombone and tuba; instead, he advises that two horns be placed an octave above the tuba. Remember always the inherent tonal weight of the instrument: in most cases it is advisable to mark it one dynamic degree below the other instruments. The protrusive quality of its tone should never be ignored, since this constitutes a factor which often results in faulty balance.

The higher tones, too, present this aggressive quality, and are mainly used for characterization. Doubled in unison with trombone, the tuba is likely to dominate and coarsen the effect, unless the dynamic is soft.

The tuba is capable of a surprisingly clear and alert staccato, if not set too low. In the middle and upper registers, its powers of articulation are formidable. An instance (very rare) of flutter-tongue appears in Honegger's *King David*. It need not be imitated.

The breath factor, very real with all brass, becomes increasingly acute with the largest instruments. Rests and curtailed phrases are imperative for the tuba, especially in strong dynamics.

The tuba mute is occasionally used by Strauss and other moderns. Its effect must be judged at performance.

In dynamic schemes not exceeding *mezzo forte,* the tuba is apt to mix better with the string basses than do the trombones. Its quality is round, lacking something of the edge of the smaller instruments. In *forte* the tuba is likely to separate from the ensemble, its egotistic quality being magnified and coarsened. In *piano* the lower octave has a beautifully matt, velvetlike quality.

A curious example of glissando for tuba occurs on page 59 of Strauss's *Don Quixote*.

Tenor tubas have been successfully used, mainly by composers of the German school. See the scores of Wagner, Bruckner, and Strauss. In Bruckner's Eighth Symphony the fifth and sixth horns double on tenor tubas, the seventh and eighth horns on bass tubas.

PHYSICAL CHARACTERISTICS OF THE BRASS

The horn, cornet, and tuba are mainly conical in shape, the trumpet-trombone group largely cylindrical. A cup-shaped mouthpiece is used by all brass except the horn; the latter's tapered mouthpiece contributes much to its dark and somewhat languid quality. The cup mouthpiece has been applied to the horn, resulting in the instrument known as the mellophone. It is a shorter tubing, easier to play, and inferior in beauty to the French horn.

THE BRASS ENSEMBLE

All suggestions given for the group use of woodwinds apply with added force to the brass family. Admirably cohesive and balanced, the latter group tends to form an island of power in the orchestra. It behaves as a unit, and its musical action is generally clearly perceptible.

This tendency towards isolation, at once a virtue and a danger, makes it imperative that all part writing and harmonic constructions be justly and sensitively handled. Dissonance—always intensified between related instruments—becomes increasingly pressing where the brass is concerned. Traditional procedures, such as prepared dissonances resulting in suspensions, emerge with superb effect. Unusual procedures, especially where the extreme registers are concerned, will bear careful checking.

Dissonance set low is likely to have a disconcerting result, as are all close constructions in the deep part of the instruments. But they may be excellent in soft dynamics.

The pattern of the overtone series, with its clear octave at the bottom, is the safest scheme to employ in distributing chords. In general, the low part of the brass is fraught with acoustic perils, bringing cloudy and dense results. The medium segment yields a pure, ringing resonance. The acute registers have a cutting brilliance which imparts tension and vitality to the musical scheme. But these altitudes mean strain for the player; for this as well as artistic reasons, their use should be confined largely to moments of intensity.

Modern examples of sonorous brass writing will be found in Hanson's Fourth Symphony and the Prelude to his *Merrymount* Suite; also, in the first Interlude from Britten's *Peter Grimes*. See, also, the superb Interlude in D minor, near the close of Alban Berg's *Wozzeck*.

HARMONIC BALANCE

Trumpets and trombones are nearly equal in power (the advantage resting with the trombones). These are brother types and always combine well. Horns are somewhat less forceful; two horns are often used to balance a single trumpet or trombone. But in quiet dynamics, or where the highest fifth of the horn is concerned, a single instrument suffices for balance.

Low horns are weak and usually need doubling. The tuba's natural power is often curbed, as remarked above, by reduced dynamics. Horns alone, when in close position, form finely balanced chords. They are often used in this way as a warm middle layer of sound. This resource—by now a platitude—can be strengthened by interlocking horns with the bright (trumpet-trombone) brass, or the latter can take over *sostenuto* harmonic functions with good results (see Chapter IX).

PERCUSSIVE SUGGESTION

Highly effective and idiomatic, as well as dramatic, is the quasi-percussive use of brass: sharply detached chords, *sforzando,* reinforcing string and woodwind patterns. These have thrust and color, and may occur either on or off the beat. They are often linked with timpani or other percussion instruments.

All rhythmic formulas are excellent in close position, but these should be neither too rapid nor too protracted. Regular rhythms have a better effect and are easier to play than eccentric formulas. Rests are an absolute necessity in protracted tongued passages.

The student is advised to study good models of brass ensemble. Besides those just given, see the final sections of *Death and Transfiguration, Pictures at an Exhibition* and Elgar's *Enigma* Variations, as well as Wagnerian examples. The score of *Die Meistersinger* provides a wonderful compendium of horn writing.

EXERCISES

Passages similar to those suggested for woodwind. Solo inventions for each brass type. Arrangement for massed brass of Bach Chorales and the Exposition of the Fugue in C-sharp minor from the First Book of the *Well-Tempered Clavichord.* (Transpose the latter to the more sonorous brass key of C minor.) Also: Fanfares for partial and full brass tutti. Arrangements of triads and dissonant chords in three up to nine parts in various dynamic schemes. The addition of woodwinds to brass in harmonic formulas, *sostenuto* and in rhythmic arrangements. The effect of dynamics must be weighed with utmost care in all brass writing.

CHAPTER VI

Percussion: Dry Colors

Percussion instruments have existed from time immemorial as a ceremonial element among primitive peoples and the races of the Far Eastern seas. Only within the past century has the cultured composer become faintly aware of their true potentialities. Today a vast array of instruments has been assembled: a group of such scope and complexity that its detailed description is beyond the boundaries of this book. For the percussion-apparatus forms in truth an orchestra within an orchestra. Its dry colors add lights and shadows, ringing and ominous hues to the musical palette.

We may separate the percussion into two categories: instruments of definite and of indefinite pitch. Another classification shows three main divisions (by substance): membrane, wood, and metal. We shall consider first the membrane type. Foremost among these are the kettledrums—in Italian, *timpani*.

THE TIMPANI

Until the present century the total range of the timpani comprised the octave F to F on the bass staff. Today this range may be extended to D below and A above, although a more practical range is from E up to G (a tenth).

Here are the sizes and ranges of the four drums in current use:

30-inch: range, great D to great A.
28-inch: range, great F to small c.
25-inch: range, great B-flat to small f.
23-inch: range, small d to small a.

The rôle of the timpani prior to Beethoven was largely restricted to reinforcing the brass, participation in strong tutti effects, and especially to defin ing the perfect cadence (two drums were used, tuned to the tonic and lower dominant).

This meager function was decisively enlarged by the master of Bonn. In addition to placing the dominant above when desired, he pitched the drums at various new intervals—octave, minor sixth, and diminished fifth. The famous octave tuning (F to F) in the Eighth and Ninth Symphonies was a masterly innovation.

Today mechanical (pedal) drums are coming into wide use. They enable the drummer to make an almost instant alteration of the pitch, whereas the older hand-tuned drums require a manipulation of the T-shaped screws ranged round the head.[1] In either case it is well to allow a reasonable time for a change of tuning (more time for a wide alteration), since *the pitch must be tested*. With four drums, however, the player has a wide choice, since the drums overlap in pitch, as the foregoing listing shows.

Percussionists are able to produce all rhythmic formulas throughout the dynamic range. However, it is important to realize that complex animated rhythms on the largest drums do not emerge with the clarity given by smaller instruments; they are somewhat blurred. But the roll (trill) comes superbly from all timpani, in all dynamics.

Write the trill:

EXAMPLE 48

And register the dynamic gradation with great care, since percussion mirrors the subtlest degrees of change with vivid effect. Also, the power potential of these instruments must never be forgotten; in a full *fortissimo* they are capable of dominating the combined orchestra.

VARIETY OF STICKS

The timpanist has an abundance of sticks available: sheepskin, soft lamb's wool, felt, soft and hard rubber, wood-head, rattan, sponge, plastic, glass—many of these in various sizes. Unless he is familiar with the effects produced

[1] The tone quality of hand-tuned drums is superior except for the finest German drums.

by the different sticks, the orchestrator is well advised to leave their choice to the player. Wood sticks tend to obscure clarity of pitch, especially on large drums.

In rapid writing, it is better to write figures that can be played on adjacent drums (the instruments are ranged pianowise, the large drums to the left). The drum is normally struck at about a hand's breadth from the rim. Struck near the center, the pitch becomes vague or even obliterated. A good *pianissimo* can be produced near the edge of the drum.

A particular note can be emphasized by using both sticks: the note is written either with two heads or two stems. This effect possesses startling force for an isolated *sforzando*. A roll can be executed on two drums tuned to the same pitch, or a tremolo on two drums with any interval relationship. Chords of three or four notes can be played by one timpanist holding one or two sticks in each hand; these are more effective in a soft dynamic. Or two players can be employed for chords or double rolls.[2] See (in Appendix) the *March to the Scaffold* from Berlioz's *Fantastic* Symphony; he calls for sponge-tipped sticks.

A curious use of snare drum sticks on timpani is found in Elgar's *Enigma* (final variation). The sound is intended to suggest the soft vibrations of an ocean liner's engines!

Timpani may be muffled or muted; this usually is done by placing a cloth on the head. This tends to stifle the overtones; timbre is duller and the pitch faintly blurred.

While the timpani often double the bass note of the chord form, they sometimes sound one of the other particles, or even notes foreign to the chord. The latter procedure has a certain danger in *forte*, being apt to disturb the chord balance.

The timpani bring a darker (grayish) shade to the orchestral color; the smaller drums add a clear, robust definition, especially effective with brass rhythms. The drums are best introduced at a moment that is important harmonically or thematically, with either a soft or strong dynamic. They deliver with superb effect rhythmic motives based on a few intervals.[3]

[2] In the "Pandemonium" of his *Damnation of Faust,* Berlioz calls for four kettledrummers (see Appendix, Ex. 22.).

[3] There is an unforgettable passage near the close of Puccini's *Madama Butterfly;* just before the heroine's suicide an *ostinato* is begun on two drums, on the open fifth B-flat and F. The effect is terrifyingly somber.

Here are a few modern examples of virtuoso writing:

Stravinsky, *Sacre du Printemps*
Shostakovich, Seventh Symphony
Elgar, *Enigma* Variations
Prokofieff, Sixth Symphony
Hanson, Third Symphony
Britten, *Young Person's Guide to the Orchestra;* "Sea Interludes" from *Peter Grimes*
Bartok, *Music for Strings, Percussion, and Celesta*
Bernstein, *Jeremiah* Symphony (see this use of maraccas on timpani)

Nineteenth-century examples:

Beethoven, Fifth Symphony, Eighth Symphony, Ninth Symphony
Berlioz, symphonies
Wagner, *Der Ring des Nibelungen*

The pedal drums make possible the use of glissando—a device more frequently heard in radio or theatre scoring. The pitch variance should not exceed an augmented fourth.

OTHER MEMBRANE INSTRUMENTS

While the timpani have been considered in some detail, owing to their commanding importance, only the chief characteristics of the other percussion instruments will be sketched. The student must study these instruments "from life," and by consulting players.

THE SNARE DRUM

Indefinite pitch; its tone is crisp, crackling, clear. (Its general pitch may be altered by changing the tension of the head.) Equal to all rhythmic problems and dynamic shades. Nervous and agile, it generally consorts with the smaller orchestral instruments. Principal strokes: the flam, ruff, group rhythms of all types, rolls, detached notes, rim-shot (stick placed on head and struck with the other stick, bullet-like in *forte*), sticks in air (sticks played against each other). The snares may be loosened, producing a duller sound, or a cloth laid on the head (muted): the incisive rattle is then obscured. In *forte* the snare drum comes clearly through the ensemble. When the sticks are reversed, the sound is heavy and powerful, with a darker hue.

MILITARY OR FIELD DRUM

Larger than snare drum, with gut snares and deeper sound. Not common in symphonic scores.

TENOR AND BASS DRUMS

The tenor—a beautiful drum—is a larger edition of the field drum but lacks snares; its pitch is vague. Various sticks are used: felt, yarn, wood, or plastic. The sound is somber and has a fine dark hue of funereal tinge.

The bass drum produces a very deep, indefinite note. The tone is dense and threatening (see the soft cannonlike suggestion in Berlioz's *Rákóczy* March). Immensely powerful in *forte,* for single strokes or rolls. Its brutal strength is notorious. Soft rolls cast heavy, threatening shadows over the picture. Large chamois-covered sticks or wood sticks (including snare drum sticks) are used. May be struck with rattan rake or bundle of sticks (*rute*). The wire brush is occasionally employed. The rolling thunder of the bass drum can shake the whole orchestra.

TOM-TOMS

These are tunable and come in sets made up of various sizes. Played by various sticks or with the hands. A variety known as *Timbales* is now in use.

METALLIC INSTRUMENTS (VIBRACUSSION)

GLOCKENSPIEL (BELLS)

Range: two-line G to five-line C; written usually one octave below sounding pitch. Brilliant, clear timbre; its silvery color is easily perceptible. Uses small mallets of wood or metal. May be struck with triangle rod.

TUBULAR CHIMES

Hanging metal tubes; range from small G to two-line G. Written at actual sound, they give the illusion of pitch depth. Powerful, clanging timbre.

CELESTA

Small keyboard instrument. Its metal bars have a luscious sound, which is likely to be covered in full tutti. Range from small C to five-line C; written an octave below true pitch. Affords rich mixtures with high strings and woods and with harp. Intensifies sentimental moods.

VIBRAPHONE (VIBRAHARP)

Fine, quivering, bell-like tone. Range is small F to three-line F. May be played without oscillators (with electric motor off) as deep glockenspiel effect. Soft mallets are usual. Yields glowing harmonic mixtures.

ANTIQUE CYMBALS

Small, tuned metal discs, unfortunately rare. Delicate silvery color; played clashed, agitated one against another (roll, two-plate), or with a metal beater. They come in various sizes and pitches. Substitutes: glockenspiel or tiny tuned bells. Also occasionally found: Castanet-cymbals, fastened to fingers, producing a high, metallic ring.

THE CYMBALS

Chinese or Turkish; plates of various sizes up to eighteen inches. Clashed, *forte,* they flood the orchestra with a brilliant and powerful hissing sound. No definite pitch; their confused overtones result in a noisy clash. For short effects write *secco.* Allow four measures of moderate tempo to adjust the cymbals for a clash.

Suspended cymbal is much used for a gonglike effect. It may be struck with various beaters at different parts of its diameter or at the edge (or one cymbal may be struck against a suspended cymbal). Rolls may be made with various beaters, or with one cymbal against another (two-plate roll).

GONG; TAM-TAM

Chinese or Turkish; the former is of hammered metal, while the latter resembles large cymbals. There are various sizes, even up to five feet! The pitch is usually indefinite. The heavy, quivering sound is awesome in *piano,* terrifying in *forte.* The powerful trembling in *forte* is hard to arrest. Avoid its use when the harmony changes rapidly, as it seems to drag over the chord impression. Touched delicately the large tam-tams have an extraordinary atmospheric suggestion. Often "borrows" prevailing pitch.

TAMBOURINES

Quasi-drum instruments in various sizes; indefinite pitch. The metal jingles lend a bright edge of color. May be shaken (roll), played with moistened thumb (thumb roll), or, in rhythms, struck against fist and knee. They add fine impact and dash to *sforzando* accents.

ANVILS

A set of small steel bars, with pitch semblance. Brilliant, penetrating color, played with metal beater or hard xylophone sticks.

TRIANGLE

Bent metal bar, made in different dimensions. The (indefinite) pitch suggestion is acute, penetrating most ensembles clearly. Silvery color, of scintillating brilliance when the roll is used during a crescendo.

SLEIGHBELLS, CHAINS, COWBELLS

Instruments of special character, rarely needed in symphonic scoring. The chains may be shaken or dropped.

WOOD INSTRUMENTS

XYLOPHONE

Wood bars tuned chromatically, range usually one-line F to five-line C. Played (usually) with hard sticks: clattering, dry sound; mainly used in its higher octaves. A fine example of use in *piano* occurs in the second movement of Debussy's *Iberia* (see Appendix). Written an octave below pitch (but specify notation; the same holds true for glockenspiel). Soft (yarn) sticks may be employed.

MARIMBA

Large brother of the xylophone: small F to five-line C. A darkish, resonant sound of round nature. Sticks are tipped with rubber or yarn.

WOOD BLOCKS

Indefinite pitch; they come in several sizes. Brittle, penetrating timbre. Related are "Chinese wood blocks," shaped like temple blocks: cuplike sound.

CASTANETS

The true Spanish instruments are, unhappily, not widely used. The substitute instrument employed is mounted. Equal to many rhythms and rolls. The sound is dry and penetrating.

TEMPLE BLOCKS

Brightly lacquered exotic instruments; a set of five gives impression of pentatonic scale. (Standard "hoofbeat" effect.) Rather hollow color.

CLAVES

Small rosewood bars: one is held in cupped hand, which acts as resonator when one bar is struck by the other. Full, clicking sound, often used to underline Spanish rhythms.

RATCHET

A wooden cogwheel revolves against a spring of wood or metal.

SLAPSTICK (WHIP)

Two hinged pieces of wood slapped against each other. A stunt device of startling effect.

A variety of other vaudeville-like devices exist: sandpaper blocks, slide whistle, bird calls, sirens, taxi horns, jingles, police whistles, and so on. They have little place in symphonic music. The wind machine, thunder sheet, shells, gourd, rattle, and string drum may, however, have occasional value in scores of program character. (See use of wind machine in Strauss's *Don Quixote*, quoted in Appendix.)

USE OF PERCUSSION

For the percussive instruments, the academic prescription, sanctified by tradition, reads: "The less the better." The department was contemptuously termed the "kitchen of the orchestra." Time and perception have brought an enlightened attitude. It is now more generally conceded that percussion provides a rich and flexible color means. The wonderful scale of suggestion, the tinting properties, the swift psychological appeal, and the wide and subtle dynamic scale—these properties are finally acknowledged. While percussion contributes little to the lyric aspect, its rhythmic and coloristic powers are remarkable enough to rank it as an element of poetic and dramatic enhancement.

Generally, the smaller instruments are employed with the higher lyrical members of the orchestra, while the larger ones are joined to the deeper choirs. But the reverse procedure is occasionally used with interesting results.

Instruments such as the triangle and the glockenspiel lend the most vivid highlights to the tonal scheme, producing radiant tints in the acute altitudes. Conversely, the weighty members—gongs, bass drum, marimba, large bells— yield somber sonorities for blends with the dark tones of cello, Bass, low brass, bass clarinet, and bassoons.

Rhythmic effects gain in definition and impact through the addition of the smaller and medium percussion. Rare, though interesting, is the sole use of the percussive choir (see the works of Edgar Varèse and John Cage).

In one sense the old view is correct: frequent use of percussion (especially *forte*) soon becomes banal and vulgar. But for the sensitive tone painter these instruments will prove an ally and a friend.

Among modern composers Bartók and Stravinsky have employed percussion with true awareness and courage.

THE PIANO

Contemporary composers show an occasional disposition to add the piano to the orchestral ranks. Since it is in principle allied to the percussion instruments, it will be considered briefly here. The piano's traditional rôle as rival to the orchestral ensemble has gradually changed to that of color complement; its wide palette has been incorporated into that of the orchestra.

The piano's range slightly exceeds that of the combined orchestra. Its color may be merged more or less freely with that of the other instruments. The modern attitude perhaps views the piano as a sonorous and rhythmic resource rather than as a lyric adjunct. However, melodic doublings are often found, especially in the higher and deeper areas.

The upper tones of the piano add verve and clarity: they mix vividly with woodwinds and pizzicato, with harp and with the smaller percussive instruments. The deep sounds have great power and substance, especially valuable for bell-like suggestion. In this region, fine clanging mixtures are possible with the large percussion, deep pizzicato, and low brass. The imaginative use of damper pedal widens the piano's color scheme; the *una corda* effect is a fine one in the softer dynamics.

Like other percussion instruments, the piano consorts best with the wind choirs. Its tone is too objective and precise to form a natural union with (bowed) strings. The reader is advised to observe the use of the piano in *Pétrouchka*, although here it carries out a quasi-solo rôle. Other effective examples are found in Hanson's *Cherubic Hymn,* Copland's *Music for the Theatre* and Honegger's *Judith.*

The piano has long been a member of the dance and theatre orchestra, where it has proved invaluable both as soloist and as filler for a scanty instrumentation.

THE HARP

This beautiful instrument is the sole plectral type normally employed in the symphony orchestra. Akin as well to the lyric and percussion groups, its accent is individual: pure, simple, and antique. Its sound has true distinction. Despite its fragile timbre, one is usually conscious of the harp's presence in the ensemble. Its color is lustrous: crystalline in the high register, while the deep sounds possess a dull, bronzelike sheen. The lowest notes are somewhat vague in pitch; their buzzing quality mixes well with deep percussion.

Here is the total range:

EXAMPLE 49

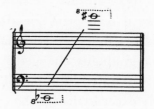

The fundamental fact to remember is that the harp is a *diatonic* instrument. Its normal scale is C-flat major. The seven pedals with which it is equipped operate upon each string of this seven-tone scale, raising the strings—*in each octave*—either one or two semitones. Thus, if each pedal is depressed to the first notch, the scale stands in C major; if the pedals are placed in the second notch, the scale is C-sharp (or D-flat) major. No further tightening of the strings is possible. Nor can the strings be lengthened below the basic scale (C-flat); hence it will be seen that double sharps or double flats, as such, are impossible. (The note D-natural, for instance, should not be notated C-double sharp.)

ENHARMONIC RESOURCES

The unique mechanism permits many notes to be tuned to their enharmonic equivalents: there are nine of these so-called homophones: for instance, D-sharp, E-flat; F-sharp, G-flat; C-sharp, D-flat. The notes D-natural, G-natural, and A-natural can be produced only on a single string (since it is impossible to raise any string three semitones or to lower a flat-string).

The pedals enable the harpist to set his strings in a variety of patterns, making available a number of modes and groupings of seven or fewer degrees. This allows him to perform the (all too well-known) glissando, by gliding the fingers across the strings. The essential point here is that all seven strings *must be accounted for*, since in glissando, the player does not skip a string. Thus the whole-tone scale can be set: B-natural, C-flat; D-flat, E-flat, F-natural, G-natural, A-natural: here the seven strings have been reduced to six *sounds* through the unison formed by the B and C strings.

It is easy also to set the strings so that four-sound chords emerge as dominant and diminished sevenths and as portions of ninth and eleventh chords.

The glissando is notated as follows:

EXAMPLE 50

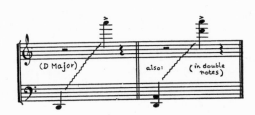

Its start and termination in the metrical scheme must be clearly shown (see example). Generally the desired notes are written as letters in the part before the passage occurs, or the scale is named. The glissando may lack sonority unless it is fairly wide, about four octaves. Always allow the player a few measures for any radical retuning. One or two pedals can be quickly changed.

BROKEN CHORDS

The harp's name comes from the word *arpeggio* (the Italian for harp is *arpa),* and the spread or broken chord is a basic technical means of the instrument. Chords are normally "rolled" unless the term *non arpeggiato* be written under the part. The harpist does not employ the little finger; thus four-part chords, in either hand, are the most idiomatic. Harp chords sound best in close position, with the chords placed in adjoining registers, and those comprising many notes are resonant and full.

HARMONICS

One harmonic—the octave of the open string—is available. The player touches the string lightly at its center with the end of the palm, and plucks it; the resulting sound is an octave higher. But the string pitch, not the sounding note, is written, with a small circle above the note. Harmonics are pure and bell-like in timbre. Their sound, being weak, must be very lightly supported. The harmonic effect makes fine colorings with high soft woodwinds or muted strings. Harmonics are effective only in the middle register of the harp's range. Two- or three-part chords may be played as harmonics *if set in close position.*

Very short effects should carry the adjective *secco* (dry); a metallic, guitar-like quality results from plucking the strings near the sounding board (notated *près de la table*).

Trills and tremolos can be played by using both hands. These effects have little power and are rarely called for, although they offer interesting color resources.

The student is reminded of the harp's strong antipathy to chromatic passages. While the pitch of the strings *can* be changed rapidly, passages founded upon chromatic patterns will not be successful unless the changes are fairly deliberate or the passage is divided between two harps.

In the last act of *Louise,* Charpentier directs the player to use a pick; the result is strange and memorable.

A final hint about arpeggios: arrange them so that one hand is not engaging the strings just quitted by the other hand. The strings need a little time for free vibration. Stretches on the harp should not be judged by piano limits: a tenth is perfectly easy.

The modern French masters provide numerous examples of fine harp writing.

EXERCISES

Solo and group passages in various tempi for the chief percussions, especially kettledrums, using both hand-tuned and pedal instruments. Experiments in mixing allied and opposed timbres and rhythms (for instance, celesta and harp, timpani and tenor drum, soft snare drum and xylophone). Harmonic mixtures of various types: piano, glockenspiel, triangle, suspended cymbals; gongs, bass drum and timpani; harp, xylophone, and soft cymbals. Invent other combinations of definite and indefinite pitch instruments.

Examples of percussion usage and passages for harp will be found in the Appendix.

Part Two
From Line to Color

CHAPTER VII

The Sketch

EVOLUTION OF THE MUSICAL DESIGN

Music is perhaps a mingling of all arts. It shares, on its own terms, their qualities and aspirations. We have dwelt—and shall dwell further—upon the sympathy that unites orchestral thought and painting. Deep also is the correspondence between music itself and architecture.

Pater has described architecture as frozen music. In its special and mysterious dimension, music too is a structural art. Like the architect, the composer must foresee the future building. He is planner, designer, and decorator. Tone is his material, and its patterns result in Form, the harmonious sum of all ingredients.

Orchestration is the servant of Form. Its function is to illuminate and strengthen tonal structure. It is a means, not an end. It needs imagination and discipline. Color is its province: color which flows, at least partly, from the sense of design and balance.

A good score rests on clear draughtsmanship. From the first tentative study to the last "realized" version, it follows a sure course.

Before painting comes drawing. The composer usually begins with a sketch —sometimes with no more than a few random ideas. These are the germinal ingredients: the inflammable materials. They represent a mood, or its beginnings. (And without mood nothing will be done.) The ideas sort themselves, circulate, and bear offspring.

At this time of gestation the composer is, consciously or not, preoccupied with the problem of design: the relationship and integration of his ideas. He is more concerned with invention and structure than with finish or color.

However, in works of special character—dramatic, impressionistic—the process may be reversed: color may be ascendant from the first impulse. A single timbre, such as a bell note, may set the mood.

THE MUSICAL SCAFFOLD

The design, or musical scaffold, should be as concise as possible. Three staves often suffice to express the first intentions, and a few clues to the instrumentation are apt to appear. It is essential to compose as freely as possible, jotting down only the essential melodic thoughts together with a few indispensable harmonies and counterpoints. (See the *Notebooks of Beethoven,* edited by Nottebohm.) The artistic course is being plotted, the main areas blocked in and shaded. To vary the comparison, we might describe this as the ground-clearing stage, the bulldozing process. The site is being leveled and surveyed. (The sketch process is excellently revealed in the extract from *La Mer,* used as frontispiece.)

Scoring should constantly support design. It is the clarifying agent, bringing into relief the salient patterns and details, revealing structure at its vital points. To cite a familiar procedure, a change of instrumental color helps to define a new theme, phrase, or section. This principle of contrast is basic in the tonal scheme. It may be carried out through alternation of choirs (antiphony), by change of solo instruments, or through counterpoints assigned to new colors. Tchaikovsky's success as orchestrator rests largely on this simple method. He scores clearly and boldly, with vivid interplay of structure and color.

SECONDARY STAGES

Following the initial sketches, the composer often carries out more finished studies before working in full score. Here let it be emphasized that the ultimate stage—the scoring—is no mere mechanical process: it is the *final realization of the music itself.* True orchestral music is *composed for orchestra.* In the act of scoring, the composer, standing before the instruments, finds his full stimulus. When the scoring stage has arrived, the structural problems have been thoroughly pondered. Details, points of color are added. The materials are brought to their highest level: equilibrium is achieved. It is a campaign, and victory depends on winning this, the last battle.

The following fragments, from the author's chamber opera *The Veil,* based on a libretto by Robert Lawrence, show three brief passages, in sketch form and in final orchestral version. The first presents a solo tenor voice supported by a light, rhythmic background; the problem is one of delicate color and texture. A whirling figure was invented with the verbal reminder "pearly color," to suggest the springlike mood of the text. A counter-motive appears at bar 4, using soft, "clanging" intervals: open fifths.

EXAMPLE 51

Rogers: *The Veil* (sketch of tenor aria)

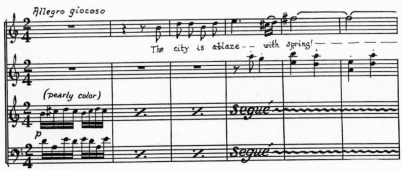

The final version (given below) shows some radical changes. The tonality has been altered, for the sake of the tenor tessitura and to place the instruments more favorably. These are points of great importance. Horns have a rhythmic-harmonic function at three-beat intervals; theirs is the main sonority. Flute and clarinet share the weaving figure, reinforced now and then by harp in shifted octaves. Strings contribute subdued but active motives. Piccolo, muted trumpet, and glockenspiel add bright points of color. Note the alternation of medium viola and high cello. While there is incessant variety, the broad mood is sustained by play of rhythm. The slender texture is abundantly lightened by rests. At the opening, high tones of piccolo, triangle, harp harmonics, and plucked violins set the gay mood with a single stroke. (The first bar of a work must capture an audience!)

The alternation of flute and clarinet, instead of employing two instruments of the same type, is due—at least in part—to the limited instrumentation. Single woodwinds only are available, except in the flute family, and here the piccolo is already in action. Necessity constantly dictates such procedures, and sometimes the result is superior to more orthodox methods.

EXAMPLE 52

Rogers: *The Veil* (realization of sketch of tenor aria)

Our second example shows the first sketch of the opera's love duet. Over a murmuring triplet figure a few motives are announced. In the fifth measure appears the tentative germ of the love motive.

EXAMPLE 53

Rogers: *The Veil* (opening of love duet; sketch)

The final version, reached after several revisions, shows great simplicity. The love motive has been defined and is assigned to solo horn: it lies in the finest region of the instrument. The background—or underground— is given to interlaced rhythms of violas and cellos supported by divided basses, with a soft, deep harp chord to launch the movement. Note how, in bars 5 and 6, the clarinet colors the horn sound. At bar 7, with the thematic answer in oboe, the second horn is given a deep pedal note. The harp returns, now borrowing the viola's earlier rhythm, while the clarinet sounds its deepest tones. The background colors are veiled, and against them the solo tenor, horn and oboe stand forth distinctly.

EXAMPLE 54

Rogers: *The Veil* (realization of preceding sketch)

EXAMPLE 54 (continued)

Our final extract presents a problem in sonority. It occurs near the close, and climax, of the same duet. Since the orchestra is very small (it needs only nine winds, besides strings, harp, and percussion), the task was to achieve a glowing effect with slender means.

The sketch consists only of a basic harmony supporting the compactly filled octave theme, illustrated in Example 55. Only the slightest harmonic clue is given in the bass part. This is later elaborated through various interlacing rhythms and color mixtures; divided cellos and Basses, harp, and bassoon. Meanwhile, the principal love theme has been added as counterpoint, being confided to the massed violins and flutes in their highest region.

EXAMPLE 55

Rogers: *The Veil* (sketch for love duet—later section)

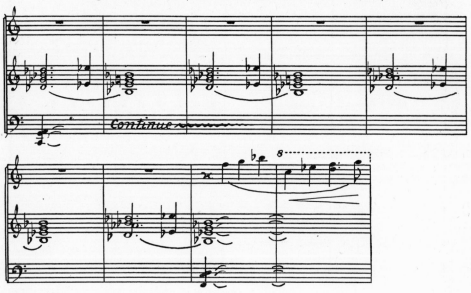

In the orchestral expansion the love theme is declaimed by brass quartet against the remaining instrumental forces, while the soprano and tenor maintain high B-flats. Trumpet and trombone outline the motive in octaves, horns supplying the inner sonority (bar 5 *et seq.*). At the seventh measure the instruments reach their peak; the effect of the high concert D and B-flat of the horns imparts a glowing color. Violins are set very high; violas, after bar 6, reach their acute register. The descent of cellos and basses, at the same measure, to the chord-third provides a richly vital foundation. At the same point the timpani sound an agitated rhythm, and harp is added to the texture. At measure 5 the brilliant harp and violins take up the motive, while the cellos are brought to a higher register. Note the comma in this decisive attack at the ensuing bars. At this moment all the brass instruments are in their highest, most penetrating, registers. Note that *just before* this peak point the solo soprano has reiterated her top B flat, a sound brilliant enough to pierce the instrumental ensemble.

EXAMPLE 56

Rogers: *The Veil* (compare with Example 55)

EXAMPLE 56 (*continued*)

CHAPTER VIII

The Picture: One

TEXTURES AND CLARITY

Our preceding chapter has shown how a score may grow from a few thematic stems, reaching fruition in the ultimate—creative—act of orchestration. Such a sequence enables the composer to focus first upon the emotional and inventive aspects: to evolve the formal scheme, finally binding together all thematic strands. However, the inexperienced composer is probably better advised to realize his musical intentions in some detail before reaching the scoring stage. His main task then will be to apply the planned instrumental colors to the completed outline.

Good orchestration is founded upon clear musical thought: pure part writing, effective dynamics, balanced form, lucid disposal of the harmonic means. Rimsky-Korsakoff, in his *Principles of Orchestration,* puts it thus:

There are people who consider orchestration simply as the art of selecting instruments and tone-qualities, believing that if a score does not sound well, it is entirely due to the choice of instruments and timbres. But unsatisfactory resonance is often solely the outcome of faulty handling of parts, and such a composition will continue to sound badly whatever choice of instruments is made. So, on the other hand, it often happens that a passage in which the chords are properly distributed, and the progression of parts correctly handled, will sound equally well if played by strings, woodwind or brass.

We have sought to emphasize that part writing is the crucial factor in all styles *into which lyricism enters;* it is the anatomy of the eventual score. Musical line assumes commanding importance in the works of the later German masters, preëminently Brahms, Wagner, Bruckner, Mahler, Strauss. Their model is Bach, in whom line, and its blossom, polyphony, reach their highest eloquence.

The reader is also advised to study intently the masters of earlier periods—Palestrina, des Près, Victoria, Purcell. Such study will guide him toward

93

pure and expressive part writing. Instrumental style is an outgrowth of the earlier vocal conceptions. Time spent with the pre-Bach masters will be rewarded.

ORCHESTRAL TEXTURES

Polyphony is not the only source of orchestral texture, however. In a simpler style, the melodic burden is given to a single element, with chordal accompaniment (homophony). Such a line may appear in any region of the orchestra; *it is a serious fault habitually to place it in the soprano.*

Occasionally, the texture arises merely from a group of chords, color being the controlling factor. Or rhythm, joined to tone color, may be the animating force. In such cases, the influence of part writing may be relaxed or even negligible.

In the orchestra the spotlight is always shifting. But the texture and style ever remain clear.

We return to part writing, with the reminder that a score usually rests on a few *real* voices. The remaining lines result from doubling. Octave doublings are constantly in evidence. Most frequently doubled are the soprano and bass, but any voice may be duplicated at the octave. In Example 57 the three upper voices are reproduced at the octave above, while the bass is doubled below.

Observe that in the fourth chord—a dominant seventh in first inversion—the bass note does not appear in the upper parts. This is usually the case with first inversions, and especially, as here, when the lowest note is the leading tone. But for purposes of special brilliance, the third may appear also in the upper parts; this procedure needs skillful handling.

PARALLELISM AS MODERN PRACTICE

The tendency to reproduce chord groups at the octave, or even double octave, is not uncommon in recent music. It is characteristic of both Ravel and Debussy, who thus achieve ample sonorities spread over much of the orchestra. Such doublings often occur within family choirs, divided strings and woodwinds being favored. A fine, clear timbre results when the lower chords are assigned to brass doubled above in woods, as in Example 58.

In such duplicated part writing the bass is rarely permitted to cross the tenor. When it does, the acoustic effect is strange, as in the extract (Example 59) from Grieg's *Peer Gynt* Suite (octaves resulting in crossing of all parts).

EXAMPLE 57

EXAMPLE 58

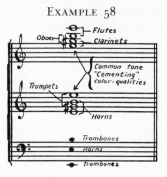

EXAMPLE 59

Grieg: "Ase's Death" from *Peer Gynt* Suite, No. 1

Here all the voices are doubled at the octave, forming a ten-part texture. The muted strings, played *forte,* have a poignant effect, especially in the dissonant chords. Bass crosses tenor at bar one.

RATIO OF DOUBLINGS

The textbook rule is a safe one in traditional writing. The root is most frequently doubled; next in order, the fifth, then thirds, as in the overtone series. Least doubled are dissonances and the leading tone. (Bach doubles the third frequently.) And in polyphonic passages, the musical logic (expressivity) of line transcends other considerations. Eloquence takes precedence over science.

It has been suggested that close writing in the deeper areas is hazardous. The rule holds for most styles, but it is sometimes contradicted where an unusual coloring is required. (See the extract from the *March to the Scaffold,* quoted in Appendix Example 8. Here Berlioz evokes an ominous, sultry atmosphere through thick spacing and heavy colors.) The end justifies the means; the mood governing certain situations verifies abnormal procedures. Art is nourished by experiment; but sensation for its own sake is stillborn.

UNUSUAL DOUBLINGS

Art seems at times to retrace its steps in order to advance. Thus the ancient device of organum has (as suggested above) given a plastic resource to contemporary composers. Parallel writing today draws upon virtually all intervals. To the consonances have been added fourths, fifths, sevenths, seconds, ninths, tenths, and twelfths; in fact all intervals form potential doublings. These are coloristic devices, piquant in effect, and resembling certain organ mixtures. Their effect can be of unique charm.

One is confronted today with the question, What is dissonance? The answer is about as easy as the definition of truth.

However, taking the traditional view, we may say that the smaller consonances, thirds, fourths (?), fifths, and sixths, sound well (smooth) in similar tone colors. Dissonances (such as seconds and sevenths), given to the same family sound curiously pungent, especially in strong dynamics. Wide intervals (twelfths, thirteenths, or double octaves) are often assigned to different types. Their effect is strangely hollow and disembodied between instruments of the same family, as in the passage from *Pétrouchka* illustrated in Example 60. Here clarinet and bass clarinet play in double octaves:

EXAMPLE 60

Stravinsky: *Pétrouchka* (page 79)

An instance of quiet doubling at the twelfth between clarinet and piccolo is given in the Appendix Example 16, *The Warrior*.

Oboes and trumpets especially lend a spicy quality to small intervals such as seconds, fourths, and fifths.

Strings also give interesting results in unusual doublings. In general, distant duplications appear as reflections, bright or faint, of the principal line, like a luminous arc of color. Here is a strange doubling—solo Bass and piccolo—at five octaves' distance; it is taken from the author's cantata *A Letter from Pete;* faintly broken rhythms of small strings and drums give a nervous inner current, marking the mood of unease:

EXAMPLE 61

Rogers: *A Letter from Pete* (Prelude)

The sound is ghostly in tint; the remote tones of the solo instruments are reconciled by the inner parts.

Opposite in principle is the next example, from Stravinsky's *Fire Bird*. Here the chord particles are tightly compressed; the sonorities, built of twin tone colors, are vividly striated.

EXAMPLE 62

Stravinsky: *Fire Bird* Suite (page 77)

GRAPHIC SUGGESTION

Another picturesque practice is found at the opening of Act III of Puccini's *La Bohème*. Two flutes and a harp play a descending passage in empty fifths, over a double pedal in deep strings. With these simple means, Puccini paints a wintry morning at the Paris custom-gate. The bleak sounds have a suggestion of sheer coldness.

In the same composer's *Tosca* there is another fine example of scene painting: the Prelude to Act III, in Lydian mode. The starry Roman night is beautifully depicted by horns, high violins, and woods; and the pealing of many bells enhances the poetic mood.

The methods described arise in the school of Impressionism, which is discussed at length in a later section.

CHAPTER IX

The Picture: Two

HARMONY AND THE WINDS

Without an understanding of the relative volumes and inherent powers of the several choirs, successful balance cannot be achieved. The question has been touched upon in earlier chapters; we shall now examine it in detail.

The natural strength of the choirs follows this order: Percussion—Brass—Strings—Woods. In numbers, brass and woodwind are about equal; but the former is potentially far stronger in volume, and this power asserts itself massively as the dynamic level grows.

Strings are individually weaker than woods and brass, but they outnumber each choir four to five times.

Percussion is the most complex, as well as the most powerful, grouping.

Strings form the most homogeneous family. Nearly as cohesive are the brasses, comprising two nearly related types. Woods include three types, forming a complex group, ideal for lyric expression and delicate tints.

The above categories show that special care is needed for the favorable disposition of the wood family. The student should acquaint himself (aurally) with the qualities and volumes of the various registers. He is reminded that the double reeds are strong and somewhat rough in the deep registers, thin and pinched in the high. Flute and clarinet are charged with dark color but are apt to be obscured in low registers. They increase in strength and brilliance as they approach the higher areas.

CHORD BUILDING IN WOODWINDS

These matters are of first importance in chord-building, especially when the woods are used alone. All conflicts of register and departures from the traditional order (flute, oboe, clarinet, bassoon) must be justified by the musical situation. But the fact that the clarinets were the last woodwinds to join the symphonic orchestra is no good reason for placing them habitually below the oboes. On the contrary: the notes on the staff define most of the finest area of the oboe, while the same notes of the clarinet include the break and contain some of the less colorful sounds.

Many of the basic questions of woodwind distribution have been outlined in Chapter IV (to which refer). We shall emphasize here that interlocking is the best practice when a fused tone quality is desired. Further, that tone color becomes more complex as more types are combined (the purest color springs from single-family mixtures). An instrument should not be placed in an extreme register when its companions are normally disposed—unless the specific goal is to isolate a chord particle or to accentuate dissonance. (Read again the remarks on dissonance and tone color.)

WOODS PLUS STRINGS

When opposed to the other choirs, harmonic woodwinds have little force. They can be singularly fine alone; see the opening chords of the *Midsummer Night's Dream* Overture and of *Scheherazade:* these clear, soft colors have a magical sound—as was their authors' intention.

Joined to string harmonies the woods add depth and fullness. Often they are used to supply notes missing from the strings when the latter are in open position. This is more effective in soft dynamics.

Another interesting arrangement is the placing of upper strings at a distance from cello and bass, the woods filling the middle region. This scheme is appropriate for soft chords.

The pedal device is likely to be given to the penetrating oboe tone, either as a single note or octave. When a held tone or chord is used, a simultaneous moving pattern should be set in *contrasted* color; here there are tremolo violins:

EXAMPLE 63

Devices employing foreign notes—scales, appoggiaturas, arpeggios, changing notes—are often given to different tone colors (Example 64b). This procedure ensures clarity in both planes. A curiously expressive effect also results from the use of *similar* colors for stationary and auxiliary notes. The quality is poignant: intimate in soft dynamics, penetrating and harsh in *forte* (Example 64a).

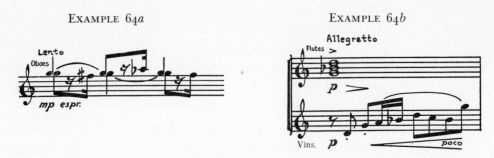

EXAMPLE 64a   EXAMPLE 64b

Dissonances removed by an octave are much milder than those in close position.

OTHER ORNAMENTAL DEVICES

Woods are often used ornamentally against sustained tones of the other choirs. Here they enliven the trumpets:

EXAMPLE 65

A string melody in octaves may be filled in rhythmically with woods; when the melody is played *forte,* the woods should be doubled or tripled:

EXAMPLE 66

(See the remarks on jazz scoring in Chapter XII.)

Correct progression sometimes results in note doublings. In such cases good part writing is usually the decisive factor (Example 67a):

EXAMPLE 67

The woods may be used for short *sforzando* accents against sustained chords in other families. But this rôle is more likely to be assigned to the stronger brass or strings.

It is worth repeating that when scoring inversions of dissonant chords, including the diminished seventh, the bass tone is usually omitted from the upper voices. The same holds true for triad inversions. Here is an example from the *Haydn Variations* of Brahms in which the second oboe resolves abnormally in order to escape from doubling the chord-third which occupies the bass part. Brahms—the purist—has led the augmented fourth into a perfect fourth!

EXAMPLE 68

Brahms: *Variations on a Theme by Haydn* (page 2)

BRASS HARMONY AND BALANCE

The foregoing remarks apply with added force to the brass choir. These rich timbres demand most careful checking of part writing and dissonance. Good spacing (the order of the overtones) is imperative. The best balance results when the instruments involved play in corresponding registers. In other cases, the group occupying an extreme register will predominate.

Interlocking brings strong cohesion; superposition often imparts extra brilliance.

EXAMPLE 69

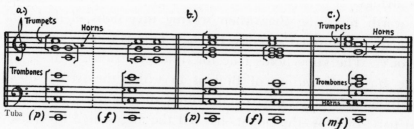

a. Interlocking: full, rich mixture.

b. Superposition: more "separated" tone; the trumpets in pure color vividly define the high third.

c. Superposition plus "cementing" of choirs: clear, sonorous blend.

Low chords in close grouping are dense and clouded, but have a fine color in soft dynamics:

EXAMPLE 70

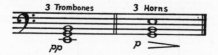

In short *sforzando* effects, the brass takes on a percussive quality suitable for violent, dramatic suggestion.

All brass instruments form excellent pedals, either *forte* or *piano*. Horns are most frequently used (usually solo or as octave pedals), and a single soft horn will provide a fine inner binding. Trumpet octaves are arresting in all dynamics. Trombone pedals are effective, but are less commonly employed.

A favorite placing of the brass pedal is in the medium-high register. However, low pedals have a fine, somber sound—rough in *forte*—while at the high extreme the ringing color stands out in telling fashion.

The pedal is often used as tonal binder, or cement, when the orchestra builds from small to large sonorities, or when the reverse process is in use. In the first case, instruments must be added skillfully to the ensemble—often a beat or so before they are needed in the harmony; while the strongest instruments are the last to enter. The important matter is to introduce or to subtract instruments logically.

BRASS JOINED TO WOODS

The high brass loses brilliance when doubled in unison by woodwinds. Its tone becomes thicker but less incisive. Some of the flashing edge is lost. Increased brilliance results when woods are added *above,* with one or two of the upper border tones doubled for a better fusion:

EXAMPLE 71

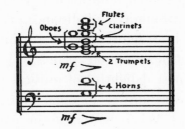

Placed thus, the woods enhance—and sound like—vivid upper partials of the brass.

Joined to deep brass, woodwinds add fine dark shades, softening the slightly coarse-grained brass timbre. They are often added to a difficult brass passage for the sake of security. The result is comforting: the brass player gains assurance.[1] The value of the psychological factor can hardly be overstated in the case of brass instruments.

SUBSTITUTIONS

A pattern that presents difficulties of range, dynamics, or articulation for a brass instrument is often given to a woodwind. If the passage is inherently brasslike in nature, the listener, by association, is likely to believe that he is hearing brass tone. But such substitutions are often employed for artistic reasons. The composer deliberately plays upon the listener's sensibility, stirs

---

[1] The unison of clarinet and high trumpet introduces the possibility of the woodwind being sharper than the brass instrument, especially when the B-flat trumpet is used.

the imagination by the subtle choice of an off-shade instead of an everyday coloring.

Strauss follows this artful course at the opening of *Don Quixote*. The first motive—so strongly trumpetlike—is assigned to the warm, full mixture of low flute and oboe. These sound the note of chivalry, but dulled, as though echoed in the misted mind of the Knight. The imagination is enchanted; and the trumpet remains in reserve.

See also the serene passage near the close of *L'Après-midi d'un faune*. Debussy replaces a third muted horn with the warm, veiled notes of the violin G-string—a true inspiration!

Similar examples are numerous, especially in music of romantic character.

SPATIAL SUGGESTIONS

The device of substitution has additional virtues, among them being the power of suggesting both proximity and distance. Woodwinds or strings are often employed to answer brass figures. When set in quieter dynamic levels, they appear to come from more remote planes. This play of dimensions is one of the simplest and most delightful of musical illusions. A similar principle employs muted brass as answer to open brass (echo), or muted brass answering woods or strings. What matters is the nature of the passage, and the means used to carry it out. Imagination does the rest.

Substitution, like invention, is often the child of necessity. In limited orchestras it is indispensable (see Example 52). Where two horns only are available, a pair of bassoons is commonly used to complete a four-part chord. Clarinets may be similarly used, but they blend less aptly with brass. Such mixtures are most successful at soft dynamic levels when the brass is placed in normal registers. The distribution of the instruments needs calculation. In a dissonant chord the sensitive interval should be given to the weaker instruments, the woods; or the dynamic level of the brass stepped down at least one degree:

EXAMPLE 72

(In *forte,* clarinets may be joined in unison to the bassoons.)

COMPOSITE BRASS COLORING

The brasses mix splendidly at the unison, either in melodic doubling or in chord mixtures, despite the fact that contradictions of register between choirs are involved. Such chord unions are compact and powerful; in *piano* the result is mysterious:

EXAMPLE 73

In *forte,* as this mixture is usually employed, the tone has immense strength, being opaque and richly vital. The mixture of low trumpets and high trombones is finely assisted by the tones of the medium horns (note that the triad root has been doubled in the horns).

Partial doublings often yield a rich effect in full brass ensemble, as is shown at the opening of Ravel's orchestration of the Moussorgsky *Pictures at an Exhibition.* Comparison with the piano part shows the horns reinforcing the trumpet-trombone strands; first and fourth horns move in octaves, occasionally adding a completing tone to the original sonority.

HARMONY IN MOTION

Wind chords may be given various rhythmic forms. For brass, the chords should be set in close position and middle or high register. Rests are essential to facilitate articulation. The chords should not move too fast, nor should they continue over a long period, unless well relieved by rests. Placed high and in *forte,* they soon prove exhausting. The same is true, though in a lesser degree, for woodwinds.

A regular (symmetrical) rhythmic pattern is easier than one that pursues an eccentric design. Sixteenth notes at *allegro moderato* form a fair speed limit. For a passage that is slightly fast for the oboe's comfort, see the close of the "Firefly" Minuet from Berlioz's *Faust.*

Rapid motion in low woodwinds is usually unsatisfactory unless confined to brief, isolated rhythms or simple weaving figures. In brass, the deep registers are muddy and relatively sluggish, while the very high regions are exhausting and protrusive. Rapid rhythms are often simplified, for playing purposes, by alternating players during the course of a figure:

EXAMPLE 74

Shock rhythms, set in dissonant forms, are sometimes given to brass. Their effect is percussive:

EXAMPLE 75

Their quality is attenuated and bitter when the brass is muted. Such color clusters are sometimes placed in woods or strings for biting color effects. In high registers the effect is vehement, while at the deep extreme the sounds are grating and coarse.

CHAPTER X

The Picture: Three

HARMONY AND THE STRINGS

Strings present fewer harmonic and coloristic problems than do the wind groups. But they are subject to the same obligations: the part writing must be lucid, the chords laid out logically. Their ample numbers allow the strings to be divided in greater or less degree. (In the *Swan of Tuonela*, Sibelius sets out sixteen string parts.) Such subdivision results in fine transparence, but at the price of reduced sonority. Elaborate textures are best suited to subdued dynamic schemes.

The rich string palette presents a wide scale of tints suitable to all harmonic formations. Set closely in the deeper registers, a somber sonority is produced, robust and heavy in *forte* and warmly expressive in *piano*. The plangent opening of the Prelude to Act III of *Tristan*, illustrated in Example 76, is laid in this region. Observe the lovely dissolving effect of the rising violins.

Two other superb examples: the first bars of Tchaikovsky's *Pathétique*, mingling the deep viola and Bass colors with the heavy notes of low bassoon; and the gravely beautiful prelude to Act III of *Die Meistersinger*.

The upper band of the spectrum is rich in fine examples of sensitive string-painting. Recall the opening of the Prelude to *Lohengrin*: against a pale blue sky the traceries of high violins ascend like fragrant smoke. Finely set for the same instruments, although very different in mood, are the Introductions to *Traviata* and *Aïda*.

The use of harmonics extends the string palette, adding soft tints of luminous quality. (For good natural harmonics the open strings must be well in tune.) Such chords are often divided in many parts; they gain substance and definition through the addition of high woodwinds. A curious result arises from using string harmonics and high woods, both playing different chord particles.

EXAMPLE 76

Wagner: *Tristan and Isolde,* Prelude to Act III (opening)

UNUSUAL VOICING

When violas or cellos are placed above the violins, the normal balance is disturbed. This method should be reserved for occasional expressive moments: it imparts intensity to a particular chord or lyric strand. In harmonic situations its effect upon the chord particle must be carefully judged. The cello first string will penetrate and separate from the ensemble, especially if assigned to a dissonance, when the other instruments occupy neutral registers.

Two departures from the normal are shown in the following extract from Mozart's Symphony in D (K. 504). The violas and second violins are placed between the cello and basses, producing a thick texture. The device is palliated by the pedal effect of the bass part. The two violins are very widely spaced until the end of bar 3; they then converge to accentuate transient chromatic modulations. The filling parts in winds and timpani are not shown.

EXAMPLE 77

Mozart: Symphony in D (K. 504), page 38

On rare occasions the Basses are placed above the cellos. It is difficult to balance their vague tone color against the clearer shades of the other strings. The device may succeed at soft dynamic levels, but its use is justified only for unusual dramatic suggestion or by some rare contrapuntal logic.

A fine resource, too little appreciated, is the use of the Bass (natural) harmonics. These are plentiful and emerge clearly. They impart to higher chord mixtures a fine, misty quality. Ravel made good use of these timbres, although his notation is sometimes ambiguous.

STOPPING AND TONE PROGRESSION

Multiple stopping is frequent in modern literature. In laying out stoppings the basic consideration is usually playability. The part-writing factor has minor importance, especially since such chord groups are often interspersed with rests—as they should be. Open strings add to the resonance and facilitate chord execution. Chords are normally played *forte,* down-bow; they sound tame in *piano.* Pizzicato chords are of fine effect in massed strings. Example 78 reveals powerful accent strokes in *Scheherazade.*

EXAMPLE 78

Rimsky-Korsakoff: *Scheherezade* (page 52)

This quasi-percussive effect mixes well with all other choirs.

(Pizzicato chords may be used to good effect in both soft and loud dynamics; they are generally more convincing in substantial dynamics.)

The student should also consider the curious *ad libitum* strummed passages in the same work. An example begins on page 83, miniature score: the strings accompany a solo for high bassoon. Also, in the same work, the powerful plucked chord on page 132, using many open strings.

To summarize, stopping adds sonority and force to the string choirs at the expense of tonal purity, refinement, and expression. When the latter qualities are needed, division is the best solution.

ANTIPHONAL WRITING

Antiphonal writing is simple in principle and brings clear results. Its vivid effect when employed between choirs is familiar, especially from the works of the Russian composers. We cite in the Appendix a brilliant usage from the *Fantastic* Symphony of Berlioz. The principle may also be carried out between groups of strings. Antiphony has many virtues, not the least of which is the exploiting of the tonal primaries (pure colors). Its values were well understood by the classic masters, and by none better than Beethoven. Like all striking effects, its power is diluted by over-use. Tchaikovsky was over-addicted to this device; in his writing it becomes a mannerism. It goes back, of course, to his rather naïve manner of conceiving music.

VARIETY AND EXPRESSION

Polyphony is the purest and noblest means of achieving expressive color in the string choir. It is the subtlest resource, the avenue to eloquence, variety, and freshness through the beauty of line. But even in writing of nonlyrical character there are plentiful—if more obvious—means of avoiding monotony. The ease with which strings change registers permits of rapid color shifts at any moment. (But sudden leaps above the ninth position should be preceded by a brief rest.) Chord structures may leap by as much as two octaves; the effect is further heightened by accompanying change of dynamics.

When strings play multiple stops they are usually interlocked, while in arpeggio writing the parts are crossed in similar fashion. The string arpeggio can be used for color and accent against sustained winds, as illustrated in Example 79.

EXAMPLE 79

Here is another accentual color device useful in all strings at all dynamic levels (this effect is also given to woods and—rarely—to brass):

EXAMPLE 80

DECORATIONS

As suggested before, strings utilize all decorative devices with excellent effect: single and double neighboring notes, passing notes, trills, tremolos, appoggiaturas. Rapid scale or figural passages, in similar or contrary motion, develop great power and suggestion. The string groups usually "hand over" to each other by means of an overlap on the accent. See the passage at letter E, page 55, in Brahms' Third Symphony.

The short glissando (*portamento*) is interesting as a color resource, but its use courts sentimentality.

Rapid figures occurring in low registers may be simplified for the Basses.

EXAMPLE 81

CLASSIC PROCEDURES

The earlier masters consistently used strings as the basis of the musical design. (Such emphasis upon a single means can be seen in an extreme, and deplorable, form in Schumann's Third Symphony.) But they also sought to create a satisfying, if often incomplete, effect in each choir, imparting to the latter a certain logic and design. The handful of woodwinds was generally insufficient to afford a balance with the string choir, while the (nonchromatic) brass was severely limited lyrically and harmonically by its restricted note series.

The amplified orchestra of our day enables the composer to hurdle earlier limitations and to adopt means denied the classic masters. But the latters' effort to grant sufficiency and eloquence to each group, insofar as the means allowed, has much to commend it. The principle is especially rewarding in the brass section, no longer a crude and intractable voice. Brass writing should be clear and resonant; it should be full without thickness; if possible, it should be self-sufficient; it should never swamp the sonority. In a word, it must be *musical*.

EXERCISES

Set chord progressions, including dissonant formations, for full and partial tutti at different dynamics and in varying distributions. Score a number of Bach Chorales for full orchestra, changing instrumental color after the *fermatas* and double bars. Write original motives and sentences for single and combined choirs, with brief developments. Follow out the sketch-to-score procedure described in Chapter VIII.

Additional material on color and textural problems will be found in the following sections.

CHAPTER XI

The Miniature

RENASCENCE OF THE SMALL ORCHESTRA

Certain signposts of today point away from the grandiose orchestra of 1900. Verdi's counsel, "Turn again to the past," [1] has found willing adherents. More and more are composers drawn to earlier ideals: clarity, economy, expression, elegance. Oppressed by the heavy eloquence of Romantic writers, they turn to intimate methods.[2] The small orchestra is given fresh accents. Even the full symphony orchestra is set on a new footing, its style reshaped. Economics and evolution combine to produce a new orchestral speech. The 140 players of *Gurrelieder* become the fifteen of the *Kammersymphonie*. The 100 of *Sacre* dwindle to the handful of *Histoire du soldat*. The 110 of *Electra* are now the thirty-six of *Ariadne*.

There is no precise definition of the term *Small Orchestra*. It applies to the concertos of Bach and Handel and to the symphonies of Haydn and Mozart. It applies as well to the *Afternoon of a Faun* and to the *Swan of Tuonela*. In general it denotes the absence of heavy brass and percussion, together with reduction of woods and sometimes strings.[3] But its meaning lies as much in methods as in numbers. Precision and subtlety replace mass and rhetoric.

[1] He did not mean servile imitation. The remark made by Boucher to Fragonard is apropos: "My son, running after these masters the way you do, you will never see anything but their behinds." Quoted by Jacques Maroger in his *Secret Formulas and Techniques of the Masters* (New York and London: Studio Publications, 1948).

[2] But the intimate masterpiece is not lacking in the nineteenth century. Consider the *Siegfried Idyll,* which we discuss in the present chapter, and the reserved and exquisite *Childhood of Christ.* Yet both Wagner and Berlioz are grand masters of the sweeping fresco style.

[3] On the other hand, a master such as Mahler sometimes applies chamber music principles to the grand orchestra.

116

RETURN TO OLDER PRINCIPLES

Today the small orchestra occupies a borderland between symphonic and chamber music, with a partiality for the latter style. Its methods arise in the so-called Baroque era; and the half century between Handel and the more mature Haydn marks off its evolution from a polyphonic to a structural-symphonic means. As employed today the small (or chamber) orchestra returns often to polyphonic principles. Clarity is placed above sonorous color. Clean draughtsmanship supplants harmonic indulgence. Suppleness replaces muscularity. Primary colors—choir and solo—are applied for their transparent beauty.

The matter of workmanship assumes high importance. While sharing certain principles of the fuller orchestra, the small group applies them with greater discipline. Details are refined, the melodic curve and harmonic volumes are more severely tested. The intimate style calls forth more intimate methods —flexibility, virtuosity, and elaborations associated with the genre of chamber music. The small orchestra demands players of high ability: its arch enemy is mediocrity.

THE CONCERTO GROSSO

We shall cite several examples, beginning with the concerto grosso. That style combines two leading principles: competition (opposition of material and textures) and agreement—the concerted use of all elements. Stated more simply, we find as leading device the alternation of solo instruments and tutti; the composer's task being to maintain formal equilibrium between individual and massed forces. We take as a model Bach's *Brandenburg* Concerto No. 2, for solo flute, oboe, trumpet, and violin, with accompanying (*ripieno*) group of string orchestra and thorough bass. The *concertino* then, consists of four contrasted solo colors, opposed to the relatively monochrome *concerto grosso*, or tutti group of strings.

Each of the three movements displays clearly the characteristics described. The opening bars of the *Allegro* show the brilliant massing of all forces; at bar 9 there is a typical combination and alternation of solo and orchestral textures, with the trumpet adding florid figural material. (The trumpet sounds a perfect fourth upward; its high, elaborate writing is a feature of the period. The precise secret of this acute florid style is apparently lost.)

EXAMPLE 82

Bach: *Concerto Grosso No. 2 in F* (page 2)

In the quietly melancholy *Andante*, only three solos are used—flute, oboe, and violin, supported by thorough bass (cembalo and cello). The strong tone of the trumpet is excluded from the delicate polyphony; the latter, with its imitative features, places this episode in the true spirit of chamber music.

With the fuguelike *Finale*, the trumpet is restored and the brilliant juggling of textures returns.

The work is a fitting example of Bach's ensemble style, with its emphasis upon line, harmonic cogency, and shrewd manipulation of volumes. The keyboard instrument fills in and reinforces the sonorous material.

The concerto grosso forms a bridge to the Mannheim masters and to their successors, in whose works design and harmony are richly developed.

THE ROMANTIC APPLICATION

Moving forward more than a century, we find the Romantic formula for the chamber orchestra in Wagner's birthday tribute, *A Siegfried Idyll*. Written

EXAMPLE 83

Wagner: *Siegfried Idyll* (page 20)

originally for solo instruments, the work calls for eight winds, including two horns and a trumpet, and string quintet. (But it is generally performed with full complement of strings, this procedure being perhaps justified by the dynamic mastery of good string players.)

Except for two brief episodes, the strings play continuously; yet so sensitive and varied is their use that monotony does not arise. We give one quotation, which shows a terraced chordal background of small strings over sustained harmonies in woods and horns; a lower strand is given to cello arpeggios in eighth notes pizzicato. Note how the wind chord is laid out in relation to the strings; the low E-flat of the oboe is rather prominent.

The piece is a perfect model of small orchestra style: transparent, varied, and refined in all its details.

A MODERN MINIATURE

Beautiful in another way is the *Mother Goose* Suite of Ravel. So inevitable and exquisitely contrived is this colored jewel that it is hard to believe that it was originally for piano. The artist's axiom, "the most from the least," is completely demonstrated. The orchestra is modest; the ear soon adjusts itself to the slender scale of volumes. Once this is accomplished the richer passages sound forth with lucent beauty. See especially the movements "Empress of the Pagodas" and "The Fairy Garden." Reticence is richly rewarded.

The question of "scale" is of utmost importance, whether the orchestra used be large or small. All effect is relative: the influence of context is ever present. Unbridled color defeats itself by sating the listener. A few brilliant touches show vividly against a scheme of quiet shades.[4] (See the discussion of "Values" in a later section.) The deepest principle of orchestration is the tasteful deployment of colors and volumes for expressive and structural ends.

Allied to the small orchestra principle is the selection of special sections of the full complement for certain works or episodes. Among many examples of this procedure we cite the "Dance of the Sylphs" from the *Damnation of Faust* of Berlioz, and the following from Tchaikovsky's *Nutcracker Suite*: Overture, "Dance of the Sugar-plum Fairy," "Arabian Dance," and "Chinese Dance."

Works of the present day for small orchestra include scores by Stravinsky, Schönberg, Alban Berg, Honegger, Bartók, Prokofieff; in fact, almost every

---

[4] "The greatest colorists have always obtained the maximum brilliance and vibration with a minimum of colors." Jacques Maroger. *Op. cit.*

living composer has been attracted to this intimate style. But before analyzing modern examples, a careful study should be made of works by the Classic and Romantic masters. Especially rewarding are the symphonies and chamber works of Mozart, Haydn, and Beethoven.

CHAPTER XII

The Way of Jazz

There was a time when the heading might have read, "The Waywardness of Jazz." But the once carefree urchin of Basin Street has grown to be a young man of the world. The smoke and sawdust have changed into chromium fittings; the old freedoms have become a sheaf of formulas. The modern jazzman is a tired troubadour.

The essence of jazz was spontaneity. It arose as a style of improvisation. That early and healthy impulse has not quite disappeared, but it is fairly scarce. Jazz, in its several variations, has become a solid industry. It is written down and regularized; its flexibility and fantasy are more or less synthetic. There is also a jazz jargon, more purple than poetic.

Obviously, a thorough study of the jazz phenomenon would call for a separate volume. Here we can merely mention some of its features and outline a few familiar formulas.

Within its own field, jazz has made valuable, if minor, contributions to the broad art of music. These have been mainly in the regions of displaced rhythm and of color. Within these areas true jazzmen display few inhibitions, and their influence has been felt in modern music. Actually, jazz or dance-band methods belong to the style of chamber music. They rest upon virtuosity, initiative, and resourcefulness, the personal element always well to the fore. The incessant struggle for a larger rhythmic freedom is, however, tragically stifled by the tiny forms and the deadly downbeat. Houdini-like, jazz is forever gripped in a struggle to slip off its self-imposed shackles; unlike that illustrious locksmith, it rarely escapes. (The brilliant modern essayist, G. K. Chesterton, has written a piece called *On the Prison of Jazz*.)

The jazz palette is often vivid, strongly defined, superheated. In quieter moments it occasionally displays inventiveness and subtlety.

Not a few European composers have found pleasure in the trinkets of jazz, which they wear with all the grace of a monocle.

JAZZ INSTRUMENTATION

There is no standard instrumentation; but a major band is likely to include a quintet of saxophones (which double on clarinets), four or five trumpets, a group of trombones, string bass, and piano; sometimes there are added a section of higher strings and/or a guitar. These operate as "units" (so termed) carrying out melodic, harmonic, and rhythmic functions. The arrangers often utilize planar scoring: parallelism as applied to the melodic-harmonic material. Characteristic is the simple device of doubling the main tune at the lower octave while inlaying the harmonies within this narrow area.[1] Conventional part writing can hardly thrive under such restrictions; the melody is, so to speak, merely tinted—as a child might wash in outlines with flat color.

The triad form is fairly uncommon, arrangers preferring to spice the harmonies freely with added notes. Such simple methods are standard with the majority of jazz orchestrators. The use of choirs is strongly functional, and insofar as this makes for simplicity, results are bold and vivid. Its blight—and it is fatal—is monotony (the eventual fruit of all formulas).

Whether the bright brass, the saxophones, or clarinets be used, the unit scheme generally prevails. But it derives important relief from the free use of solo instruments: a single line set against moving block colors. The variation principle, intricate decorations, cross-rhythms, the spotlighting of separate colors—the whole effect steadied by simple underbeats of Bass, piano, and percussion—these form the usual resources.

COLOR EXPLORATION

In the world of color, the more sedate composer might well abstract some leaves from the jazzmen's book. As remarked earlier, snobbishness has never been the popular musician's failing. He has been quick to appreciate the extensive technical resources of instruments, especially winds. The normal upward limits have been extended, various means of vibrato cultivated, and mutes of many types placed in constant use. Tonguing has been brought to a remarkable point, given a liquid ease and grace. Hues and mixtures of brass have been expanded, ranging from softest whispers to the most strident thrusts.

[1] There is nothing new about this. Puccini, Rimsky-Korsakoff, and others freely employ it.

To the mutes named earlier are added the soft and hard hat, the wa-wa, kazoo, megaphone effect, and others. They produce shadings of strange and interesting character, although not necessarily amiable.

THE SAXOPHONES

Above all, jazz arrangers have acclimatized the saxophones. These are indeed infinitely useful instruments, and deserve recognition by composers of all ranks. We give their basic characteristics. The normal range is similar to that of the oboe: B-flat below treble staff to F above the staff. The finest players are able to carry this compass considerably higher.

Built in eight sizes, the saxophone employs this range for the *written notes*; transposition is according to the size of the instrument. The soprano, in B-flat, transposes a major second lower; alto, E-flat, a major sixth lower; tenor, B-flat, down a major ninth; baritone, E-flat, an octave and major sixth down.

In the jazz or dance band, a few saxophones of different dimensions build a warm and powerful core of tone. This is used as opposition color with the brass, as mixtures, or for lush melodic effects. Antiphonal writing is frequent and is generally highly successful.

The tone of the saxophone is rich and substantial, suggesting a composite of brass and woodwind, with perhaps a trace of viola timbre. The finest players produce a sound of smooth, expressive character, creamy and even throughout most of the range.

The instrument is a hybrid, combining physical features of the oboe and clarinet families. The mouthpiece is a single reed, the tube's shape conical, overblowing at the octave. It is relatively easy to learn, yet true virtuosos are scarce.

TECHNICAL FEATURES

Despite the full, penetrating tone, the saxophone is remarkably flexible, executing all technical material with relative ease. Its emission is fluid, resembling that of the clarinet, although the latter's tone is far more refined and gracious. It is perhaps the hint of coarseness and a certain glib facility that has conspired to lower the instrument's prestige among serious composers.

Among technical features, observe that wide upward slurs are safer than those downward, although in longer note values both types may be used. Octave skips present no problems. The subtone technique (described before) is available and is usually employed with tenor saxophone to soften the somewhat heavy timbre. In dance and radio arranging, the octave of flute or clarinet and tenor saxophone has been successfully used.

One of the chief virtues of the instrument is its strong affinity with all other types of tone color, forming a valuable transition between winds and strings. Incorporated into the symphony orchestra, its bulky timbre could fortify the now weak woodwind section. There is no doubt, however, that the saxophone's bland quality soon grows wearisome.

Numerous brilliant recordings, radio and live performances beyond count, facilitate intensive study of this scoring style.[2]

THE GOD-FROM-THE-MACHINE

The microphone has profoundly altered the listening attitudes and impressions of our modern world. It is a vast and little-understood subject, far outside the framework of this volume. The microphone is with us, and will remain with us, and its influence cannot be foreseen. The mysterious gadget transmits and magnifies, making possible bold, new effects with small economic means; that is, as far as playing personnel is concerned. It is the universal ear and reporter. The giant symphony orchestra of the post-Romantic masters is little suited to its talents. Music must adjust itself to the realities of a microphone age; already the term microgenic has been coined.

In the process of pickup and transmission, certain values are lost; the delicate upper partials disappear or become attenuated. Violin and other fragile timbres are somewhat impoverished, and many problems connected with the complex character of percussion remain to be solved. But research and experiment are constantly at work in the direction of tonal fidelity, and the level has been decisively raised in recent years. There can be little doubt that advancing techniques will contribute distinctive features. The entrance of electronics upon the musical scene ushers in a changed world. So far there is no cause for complacency; the type of radio music disseminated plus the narrow frequency range available on most commercial receivers and phonographs, as well as records, are harshly limiting factors.

[2] There is a faint, and amusing, kinship between the jazz use of piano and the *continuo* realization of two centuries ago.

CHAPTER XIII

Solo and Orchestra

Arising from the early vocal forms, the solo concerto has moved steadily in the direction of instrumental display. Since Haydn, it rests mainly on the principle of competition between individual (virtuoso) and orchestral group (tutti).

As in the parent concerto grosso, opposition of texture and color is the determining factor. But the nineteenth century enlarges the design radically along the lines of sonata form, while emphasizing the subjective side. The structure reaches symphonic proportions and becomes a field of friendly warfare between soloist and orchestra. The spirit of fantasy is given free range, problems of technique and volume are posed and solved. The capacities of the single instrument are intensely explored, and provision is made in the cadenza for the element of quasi-improvisation.

THE PIANO CONCERTO

The piano—long a favored solo medium—is well fitted to its rôle. Its color and character are individual, and these it does not surrender to competitors. (The paradox of the piano is that it mixes with everything, while it blends with nothing.) Against the sensuous timbres of the orchestra, its crisp, objective colors stand forth plainly. The piano's friendliness with winds and percussion affords distinctive groupings, and its incisive tone forms a natural foil to the warm-hued strings. Despite these native advantages, the instrument can scarcely cope with the full power of the orchestra, unless treated with skill. We list a few procedures which apply to all concerto writing.

As remarked before, contrast of color and musical material is a prime virtue. It is clearly shown at the opening of Tchaikovsky's B-flat Concerto; clangorous piano chords oppose the majestic design in the orchestra. The solo part is simple and dramatic:

EXAMPLE 84

Tchaikovsky: B-flat Concerto (opening)

Note the reduced instrumentation and dynamics against the massive solo chords.

Equally impressive is the antiphonal means, the alternation of solo and tutti textures. The extract is from Beethoven's Fifth Concerto:

EXAMPLE 85

Beethoven: Piano Concerto, No. 5 (page 61)

Another quotation from that work shows a harmonic usage of the same principle:

EXAMPLE 86

Beethoven: Piano Concerto, No. 5 (page 56)

(The thick left-hand chord of the piano part would rarely be scored thus for orchestra; the notes would be arranged in open position.)

The opening of Béla Bartók's Piano Concerto No. 3 again offers an example of direct contrast. The thematic design, spaced at two octaves, is heard from piano against a quiet weaving of strings joined by clarinets and completed by pulsations in timpani:

EXAMPLE 87

Bartók: Piano Concerto, No. 3 (page 1)

We draw further from Beethoven's Fifth Concerto, for an elaborated doubling between piano and strings. Note the clashes that arise between the designs of the first violins and the piano; the opposed tone colors give a fine poignancy to the device. The strings maintain a pattern of simple part writing:

EXAMPLE 88

Beethoven: Piano Concerto, No. 5 (page 111)

For a charming (and famous) example of piano set against woodwind, see the "triangle passage" in Liszt's E-flat Concerto.

The next quotation is drawn again from Béla Bartók's Concerto, chosen to demonstrate the handling of a harmonic texture. The difference in distribution is apparent: close horns and bassoon sound the notes of the piano left hand, but an octave above. Notice the strange mixture of tam-tam (*poco forte*) with deep piano chords:

EXAMPLE 89

Bartók: Piano Concerto, No. 3 (page 48)

VIOLIN AND ORCHESTRA

More taxing are the problems raised by the combination of violin and orchestra. As the solo color is now drawn from the chief orchestral choir, sensitive handling is needed to secure contrast when the string ensemble is present. A simple means is to plan contrast of register and rhythmic texture. We present below a group of examples drawn from Tchaikovsky's Concerto in D major.

Page 5: Solo violin plus string orchestra. The latter is placed below the solo line, and is given a simple pattern. At bar 5, first violins borrow the solo material *in a separate register:*

EXAMPLE 90

Tchaikovsky: Concerto in D (page 5)

Page 19: Thematic design in first violins and flute. Against it the soloist plays a vigorous obbligato of large span; contrast of material, texture, and color (Example 91).

EXAMPLE 91

Tchaikovsky: Concerto in D (page 19)

Page 54: Delicate rhythmic design in solo violin supported with detached chords of tutti strings, *pianissimo*. Basses at second bar only, darkening the foundation. Note group bowings—offbeat in first bar, onbeat in second—in solo part.

EXAMPLE 92

Tchaikovsky: Concerto in D (page 54)

Page 51: High solo violin in elaborated doubling of first violins, two octaves below. The brush-work of clarinet and flute adds color and action; horns enrich the harmonic tissue.

EXAMPLE 93

Tchaikovsky: Concerto in D (page 61)

See, also, opening of the *Canzonetta* from the same work. An introduction for soft winds ushers in the theme by muted violin supported by muted strings. Here again is contrast of register and material. The offbeat accents for horn and imitation by deep clarinet are noteworthy.

Further, the cadenzalike passage, page 93, showing various violin devices, and the passage on page 103, wherein low double notes of solo violin are embedded in a light covering texture of string orchestra.

OPPOSITION OF TONE COLORS

We have cited several examples of solo violin placed against massed string tone. Easier to carry out is the principle of opposed tone coloring. But it must be recalled that heavy brass will obscure solo violin, unless the dynamic is fairly soft or the solo set in a distant register. Rhythmic contrast is also effective, but even detached brass chords may be overpowerful unless the solo is strongly opposed in area and character. Percussion, too, always needs careful application. As a general rule, full tutti is employed when the soloist rests.

As additional models, we suggest the violin concertos of Mozart, Beethoven, Mendelssohn, Brahms, Saint-Saëns, Lalo, Bruch, Sibelius, Bloch, Stravinsky, Elgar, Walton, and Berg. The Classics and Romantics also prove sure guides to piano concerto style; to their works may be added modern examples by Rachmaninoff, Bartók, Stravinsky, Honegger, Ravel, MacDowell, Hanson, E. B. Hill, William Schuman, and Anis Fuleihan.

OTHER SOLO TYPES

The use of solo viola and cello raises subtle questions of balance and color. Strongly individual as they are, their timbres—darker than those of the violin —are more readily absorbed by the surrounding ensemble. Skillfully conceived methods of contrast are imperative.

The viola emerges best when its outer strings are juxtaposed with contrasted colorings. Equally indispensable is distinction of rhythm, register, and general design. The tendency of the viola to seep into the prevailing scheme of timbres must never be ignored. Excellent models for study are the *Harold in Italy* of Berlioz, the Viola Suite of Bloch, and the Concertos of Walton and Hindemith.

In the case of the cello, the distinctive A-string tone provides the clearest lyric means. (Its cloying color will not bear overuse, however.) The expressive middle strings are easily covered, while the thick C-string is depressing and is clumsy at moments of animation. Light accompaniment and strong contrasts again offer surest avenues to clarity. As models, consult the concertos of Haydn, Saint-Saëns, Dvořák, Elgar, Brahms (Double Concerto for violin and cello), Strauss (*Don Quixote:* viola and cello obbligato), and Bloch's *Schelomo* and *Voice in the Wilderness*.

The suggestions given apply with equal force to concertos for wind instruments. To summarize the essentials:

> *Contrast:*—of color, design, register, texture.
> *Balance:*—equilibrium in style and structure between solo and ensemble.
> *Style:*—solution and integration of idioms of both elements: solo and tutti.
> *Color:*—Always clarity; transparence when solo is present.

The use of occasional solo passages, as incidental effects, rests on the same methods. Strauss, Ravel, and Debussy, among others, present fine examples, including solo string colors. And the works of Rimsky-Korsakoff are lavishly adorned with solo string and wind material. See, especially *Scheherazade, Russian Easter,* and *Spanish Caprice.*

EXERCISES

Short examples for classic orchestra with solo piano or solo strings; solo woodwinds and horn may also be used, following the axioms given. A study of later models should precede practice with the modern orchestra.

CHAPTER XIV

Voice and Theatre

A large area of musical history is occupied by vocal-dramatic art. Here we shall merely touch on some of its problems as they relate to the use of voices with orchestra.

The human voice is a natural instrument, treasurable for its intrinsic beauty and for its unique ability to unite word and musical sound. Its sphere is the subjective, its communication explicit. Despite severe limitations of technique, it commands a grand range of feeling.

While the vocal timbre differs from that of constructed instruments, it is in effect the protoplast of musical expression. All other types except percussion form extensions of this first (human) model. Closest in principle are the winds, particularly the woods, while strings, too, suggest the inflections and suppleness of a skilled voice. But modern thought does not regard instruments as a substitute for the vocal organ. Occupying different planes, their relation is one of friendly accord.

The ranges of solo voices may be set as follows:

EXAMPLE 94

Falsetto extends the compasses upward by several degrees.

In choral writing (for untrained voices) the above ranges should be reduced by a third at top and bottom. Highly important is the question of *tessitura* (most frequently used area); this is generally located in the central portion of the range.[1]

AREAS OF THE VOICE

In the middle region the voice color is pure and relaxed, while the question of fatigue is reduced to a minimum. Highest and lowest segments should be reserved for moments of special expression. Their use should not be protracted.

Like other instruments, the voice shows three general bands of color: dark, natural, and brilliant. The timbre varies with the type of voice, the deeper species displaying a heavier and more somber character.

The complex questions of vowels and consonants, and of prosody and diction linked to tone production, are outside the scope of this volume. We remark merely that a good text is apt to have a minimum of sibilants while being well endowed in vowels at climactic moments. The problem of vowels, diphthongs and consonants differs according to the type of voice. Here the advice of a well-equipped singer should be taken. Also influential is the species of national language used for musical setting.

A good vocal line shows tasteful variety of level and of rhythm; it displays a clear, attractive contour. Such a line usually avoids overactivity—incessantly busy patterns—showing a certain symmetry and simplicity, and embracing a fair number of white notes spaced according to the textual sense. Vocal style is generally more restrained and direct than that of instruments. Sufficient, well-placed breathing places are essential. These are provided by commas or rests; together with slurs they define the phrasing and poetic implications.

VOICE AND INSTRUMENTS

A decided difference exists between the timbres of men's and women's voices. This question bears strongly upon the technique of scoring. As remarked earlier, wind instruments are closest in character to the voice. The small woodwinds recall female voices; bassoons and brasses resemble male qualities. (The higher cello notes often suggest the timbre of a tenor voice.) Although blending attractively with the vocal organ, all winds introduce an element of rivalry.

---

[1] For a detailed treatment of this problem, see G. F. Soderlund's *Direct Approach to Counterpoint in 16th Century Style* in Eastman School of Music Series.

Strings are the safest background and complementary colors. Against them the voice is heard in clear relief. Their transparent nature and delicate dynamic scale usually allow even the lightest voice to survive. But the principles governing all solo writing apply here as well: distinction of thematic materials, contrast in direction, careful spacing. It is true, however, that the voice's unique timbre and the textual element constitute decided assets.

A factor of some importance is the placing of the instruments. Set on stage, on the singer's level, the orchestra offers formidable competition. Placed in the theatre pit, the instruments' power and brilliance are as a rule appreciably reduced. This question should influence the scoring procedure.

THE FEMALE VOICE

The low portion of the female voice requires discreet instrumentation. Here strings are the likeliest supporting media. Low woods, unless soft and sustained, offer rather dangerous competition, except in the theatre pit. Set far in register from the voice, their threat is reduced while the contrast of colors proves interesting. Brass is usually hazardous unless softly sustained and placed beneath the vocal line. As the voice ascends, stronger hues may be introduced, but care must be taken that the general resonance does not obscure the text. A substantial voice placed in its highest region can resist massive instrumentation. But the full force of the orchestra should be rarely unleashed. A glittering tutti is usually employed while the singer proclaims a climactic phrase or sustains a peak note (see Example 56, Chapter VII). Another excellent method is to bring in the full orchestra just after the singer has attacked a brilliant tone.

THE MALE VOICE

With men's voices, the principles are largely similar. The quality is obviously stronger and fuller than that of the woman's voice, and it competes more confidently with wind instruments. But heavy brass in the same area as the vocal part is hazardous unless the voice is unusually robust and the texture skillfully contrived. Below *mezzo forte* the power of brass is considerably curbed. It is wise to avoid the top registers of these instruments.

Woods and strings offer little rivalry under average conditions, but percussion is perilous unless discreetly used. Suggestions given in regard to full tutti hold true again. Often the full force of the instruments is invoked only after the singer has closed a phrase, or as a pendant to the voice material.

DOUBLING

Doubling of voice and instruments is an effective practice. It lends security to the singer, and the color mixture is often sensuously beautiful. Women's voices may be doubled at unison or octave above by small strings or woods. (It is pertinent to recall Rimsky-Korsakoff's remark, that the flute placed in the same region as the soprano voice has little brilliance. Where it is desired to match or brighten the vocal timbre, the flute should be disposed an octave higher, that is, *above* the staff.) Brass is rarely used to double female voices except for moments of climax or when the instruments are in the theatre pit.

Any of the large instruments may double men's voices at unison; the brighter instruments are apt to associate with tenor voice. Doubling voices at the upper octave increases brilliance and incisiveness, while a more somber color results from doubling at the deeper octave.

It must be admitted that the doubling device is now rather obvious. Above all, it is inappropriate when the vocal part calls for subtle fluctuations of time (*rubato*), nuance, and feeling. It suits the straightforward line and expansive sentiment.

PUCCINI AND VERDI

Much addicted to the method of doubling was that cunning master of theatre scoring, Puccini. His clear-cut melodic formulas and sentimental contours doubtless condone this habit, which he sometimes indulges through spacings over several octaves. And for general mastery, for canniness of detail and characterization, it would be hard to name his superiors in the modern theatre. There is one. On a grander scale, made of finer metal, is the mature Verdi. The greatest Latin master of opera is a true painter; his later music is distinguished by the most sensitive strokes and boldest inventions. Such scores as *Aïda, Otello,* and *Falstaff* are treasures of instrumental and vocal felicity.

For an illustration of baritone solo with orchestra we draw upon that unjustly ignored melodrama by Puccini, *The Girl of the Golden West.* The passage is the bitter arietta of Jack Rance (beginning on page 108, full score). With fine sobriety Puccini emphasizes the quieter colors of the string orchestra, occasionally adding a few woodwinds at the unison or octave to vary or intensify the shifting moods. (His inveterate predilection for parallel progressions in fourths and fifths is strongly in evidence.)

The violins play above the staff for exactly twelve notes; horns are used only in four measures; trombones for two beats; timpani for six beats. At the brief climax, when the singer attacks a high F-sharp, violins and deep woods descend to their grave registers, attack strongly and release, while the voice sustains, solo, over a fermata. A masterly example of restraint!

A far better known passage by the same composer is the love duet in Act I of *Madama Butterfly;* a superb model of glowing and limpid instrumental color against the lyric-dramatic lines of the two protagonists.

The Flower episode near the close of Act II of the same work is a lovely example of lightly enameled colors surrounding the voices of Butterfly and Suzuki.

In Verdi's operas there are countless instances of felicitous instrumental and vocal thought—although the great Italian often tends to favor a high tessitura. Among the sunset splendors of his *Otello* is the tender and anguished ending; the words *Un bacio* are repeated with sublime feeling. Truly, we may apply to Verdi a line of Iago's: *"Ecco il leone!"* [2]

FRENCH CHARACTERISTICS

The modern French masters found a genial model in the practices of Rimsky-Korsakoff. But lucidity is a deep-grained virtue among all Gallic artists, and the nineteenth-century writers—Bizet, Auber, Hérold, Boieldieu, Offenbach, Gounod, and Saint-Saëns—provide luminous examples of theatre scoring. Bizet, especially, has the secret of apt and vivid color. His scoring is lithe and expressive; with a few strokes he is able to define locale and character. His fiction (Spain) is better than the truth.

The scores of Massenet deserve study for their surety and delicate coloring.

Always the hand of the French composer rests gently upon the orchestra. And particularly with woodwinds is his touch instinct with grace. He is at once persuasive and fastidious. (The score of *Pelléas* is a unique example of instrumental continence.)

The German Romantic school, led by Wagner, create an elaborate web of sound which needs powerful voices on the stage. This opulent orchestra, with its forest of thematic allusions and rich polyphony, reaches its culmination in the *Salomé* and *Electra* of Strauss and the *Gurrelieder* of Schönberg. These are dangerous models for the student.

[2] "Behold the lion!"

Admirable in a different key is the technique of Arthur Sullivan. His deft touch is shown in the series of operettas written with W. S. Gilbert. He does not forget the first article of theatre scoring: *Never cover the voice.*

The modern Benjamin Britten displays strong gifts for dramatic coloring in his operas *Peter Grimes, Albert Herring,* and *The Rape of Lucretia.*

Among Americans, the work of R. R. Bennett is well known for its skill and verve. His talent has enriched the arranger's art. His compatriots, Gian-Carlo Menotti, Marc Blitzstein, Virgil Thomson (adept in plastic prosody) and Douglas Moore, among others, show a real instinct for the small theatre.

CHORUS AND ORCHESTRA

Balance between chorus and orchestra raises fewer difficulties. But the general physical factors remain influential. If both groups are on stage, a large chorus is needed. With an orchestra of ninety players a chorus of 150 to 200 should be used. But too many unpredictables are involved (acoustics of the hall, especially) to warrant generalizing.

Regarding tessitura and range, the injunctions given for solo voice hold good, except that the compass is narrower, the central portion of the voices —a sixth—being mainly employed. Clear textual setting and ample provision of rests are equally essential. A broad style, using bold strokes, suits the chorus well, although a good choir is capable of many subtleties. Richness and resonance lie closer to the medium areas of the voice than to the top extreme.

Variety of texture is gained by contrasting volumes and rhythms and by ample use of contrapuntal methods. Simple procedures, such as octave doubling of men's and women's voices, come off admirably. Sustained tones against moving parts (oblique motion) is another excellent device.

Triads placed fairly high sound with gleaming brilliance in chorus and orchestra (see Appendix, Example 21 and Example 22).

MODULATION AND CUES

The question of modulation needs careful handling, although the presence of supporting instruments is strongly helpful. It is very important to provide clearly perceived cues before the choral entrances, especially in a complex harmonic scheme. Extreme registers must be used sparingly (as suggested above) and always with awareness of their relation to the poetic-dramatic demands.

As with solo singers, though to a lesser degree, restrained instrumentation is required when the low register of the voices is used. The chorus, too, is often doubled by instruments at unison and/or octave for security and color. This is recommended for difficult passages. When the full orchestra is used *forte,* the choral register should be fairly high. Contrast of material between choir and instruments can be strongly effective. But avoid overelaborate formulas and what is well-named "paper music." Simplicity and breadth are the keys to success.

An adequate demonstration can be found in the long line of familiar masterworks from Handel to Stravinsky. Brilliant models are Honegger's *King David* and Walton's *Belshazzar's Feast.* The student should consult also the well-wrought scores of the Americans Horatio Parker, Randall Thompson, Howard Hanson, Normand Lockwood, Virgil Thomson, Roy Harris, William Schuman, Herbert Elwell, Aaron Copland, Norman Dello Joio, Peter Mennin, and Lukas Foss. Richard Rodgers shows admirable mastery in the field of operetta. He has to his credit a long line of haunting melodies, and is a master of the style of wedding tone to words. Other true masters of the apt tune and mood were Jerome Kern and George Gershwin. Notably gifted for his sensitive vocal writing and delicate scoring is Samuel Barber.

CHAPTER XV

Craft of Arranging

Arranging—often colloquially called "transcription" or "adaptation"—actually resembles the process of translation. It is the craft, or art, of rescoring a musical work. The idioms of the original are interpreted in terms of the new language. The medium changes while the spirit and flavor of the music are preserved.

Principles of voice leading, volume, and design already emphasized hold good for all orchestral tasks. Interwoven now is a new value: the *style* of the music. The arranger becomes, momentarily, the alter ego of the composer. While acquiring new inflections, the artist's original accent is retained.

Orchestration is no mere decoration; its function is architectural and coloristic. Before scoring, the arranger will study the materials and structure of the original. His distribution of color masses will conform to the large design while reflecting the minor play of moods. In short, the instrumental scheme follows the musical plot. As suggested earlier, decisive changes of scoring are likely to occur at significant places in the form, especially when the sonata or variation types are involved. But the arranger will avoid incessant shifts of color—the restless, mosaiclike manner quickly breeds monotony. Moderation is ever a good motto.

PIANO INTO ORCHESTRAL STYLE

Since piano music forms the usual material of arrangement, we shall confine our discussion to that technique. One sure clue is given the arranger: *The orchestra has no pedal.* That mechanism is peculiar to the piano; it enables the player to spread and sustain tone, to suffuse the texture with a rich mist of sympathetic sound. The clash and clang of partials—satellite tones—develop warm-hued or crystalline sonorities.

The effect of the damper pedal should never be forgotten. Where pedaling is indicated, its approximation must exist in the orchestra. As a rule, the deeper instruments retain a sound for the pedaled duration; sometimes a complete chord is so treated while solo instruments carry out the melodic part. We may recall that in musical theory and practice the term *pedal* (as distinct from the piano mechanism) signifies sustained tone or tones in any area. The orchestra, with its wealth of distinct voices, is peculiarly fitted to carry forward that principle. Middle and high pedals—fairly scarce in piano style— are constantly employed in orchestra. The distinction of color now available proves an ideal asset.

The pedal effect may occur as single sound or may be doubled over one or more octaves. Instruments of penetrating color are often assigned this rôle, but all instruments are capable of such service, depending upon the dynamic and harmonic schemes. Pedals are often given rhythmic patterns, thus acquiring thematic (emotional) significance. But all deviations from the original piano material are suspect. Additions or changes must be scrupulously justified as arising from the style and spirit of the original. Harmonic tampering, such as change of position, is never permissible.

TEXTURE

The reader has seen that the overtone series is often chosen as a model for clear sonorities. In that grouping the widest intervals occur in the lowest region. On this basis thick writing for the deep instruments becomes an exceptional practice.

However, in piano style, it may happen that for physical or other reasons the left hand sounds a low chord—often detached—in close position; see the piano chords in Beethoven's Fifth Concerto, quoted in Chapter XIII, and compare these with the orchestral "answers." Such spacing would sound turbid if transferred literally to orchestra. (But, for certain curious suggestions mainly appropriate for dramatic music, such a scheme might be used, especially in soft dynamics. See the third and fourth movements of Berlioz's *Fantastic* Symphony, among many instances.) As a rule, then, deep chords are set in wider intervals—octaves, fifths, sixths, and sevenths—unless the contrapuntal procedure produces other textures.

Sometimes, for reasons of orchestral effectiveness, the orchestrator will transpose the original piano version. The key of F-sharp may be shifted up (or down) a half-step; the new key is more sonorous—including, as it does, several open strings—and is easier for the orchestral instruments. (See end of p. 152.)

PIANO VERSUS ORCHESTRAL FIGURES

Bearing on this question is the matter of figuration. Typical piano figures, especially in close position, are often remodeled. The stiff Alberti Bass, for instance, would sound pathetically dry and meager if reproduced "as is" in orchestra. Here it is shown together with an idiomatic respelling:

Alberti Bass:

EXAMPLE 95

Redesigned for strings:

EXAMPLE 96

The figure, although still in close position, is moved to a slightly higher register and is amplified. The result is somewhat thick, but is feasible, especially in soft dynamics. Cello and bass provide sustaining and accentual material.

Example 97 shows another, more open, texture. This is a tutti texture, serviceable in both *forte* and *piano*. Winds provide the sustaining factors; a much more tenuous effect would result from using the string group alone for this chord. Note that the chord particles are spread—open position—in the main string instruments, producing a transparent texture. Among the winds, certain chord-tones are doubled: see arrangement of oboes and clarinets and of horns and trombones. This yields a more compact sonority.

EXAMPLE 97

Still another example of triad arpeggio, with an added melodic fragment:
Piano design:

EXAMPLE 98

Orchestral version:

EXAMPLE 99

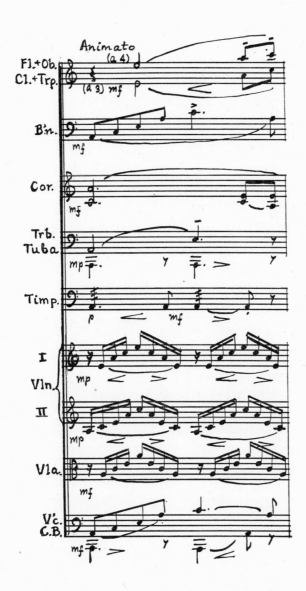

Deep instruments conform to the pedaling; cellos and bassoons play an augmented version of triad form.

ARPEGGIO WRITING

The utmost care must be taken to achieve a pure sonority, considering instrumental registers, nuance, and playability of broken chords. Strings can carry out arpeggios in all distributions, while woodwinds usually outline these in close position. Open position brings greater transparence. For more compact and opaque textures, patterns are restricted to more limited areas. Figures may pass back and forth between strings and woods, although the break in color is perceptible. The less mobile brasses are rarely used for figurations, even when the note values are fairly broad. But they often take repeated-note effects as a means of animating sonorities.

"PICTURES AT AN EXHIBITION"

The student is urgently advised to make a careful study of the remarkable orchestration of Moussorgsky's *Pictures at an Exhibition,* made by Ravel in 1923.[1]

Before giving quotations, it may suffice to remark that the French master made comparatively few additions to the original piano version. Where they occur they are necessary for sonorous, coloristic or program reasons. While remaining loyal to his model, Ravel has been unfailingly idiomatic in his translation.

Here is an example from No. 3, "Tuileries":

EXAMPLE 100

Moussorgsky-Ravel: *Pictures* (page 45)

[1] This score, carried out at the suggestion of Koussevitzky, has recently been made available in miniature form by Boosey & Hawkes. The original piano version is included.

Woodwinds only; original notes only, except for octave doubling at bar 4; but observe accents and staccato. At bar 5, pizzicato chords for accent and color.

An important point is seen in the phrasing of the woodwinds—they differ not only from the piano part, but from each other. Phrasings and string bowings are treated idiomatically, often resulting in different versions and in departures from the original details.

No. 4, "Bydlo."

EXAMPLE 101

Moussorgsky-Ravel: *Pictures* (page 45)

Almost literal rendering: Low strings, muted, played with dragging accents. Deep bassoons have legato version, second bassoon on dominant pedal. Heavy, oppressive, soft sonority. Solo part in tuba: the extreme range is dangerous. Note deep sounds for harp *when harmony changes.*

No. 10, "The Great Gate of Kiev."

Example 102

Moussorgsky-Ravel: *Pictures* (page 128)

This, the final section of the suite, deserves most careful study as a remark-able solution of a complex problem. It forms a masterly structure in sound, bold and confident, conveying in performance a richly monumental effect. The arranger's art is raised to its highest estate; momentarily Ravel and Moussorgsky become a single personality.

Contrasting of broad, vivid sonorities. Bars 4 to 7 show compact groupings in brasses rounded by bassoon tone. High woods suppressed for greater effect at reëntrance, bar 10. Here the power of full orchestra is freed. Divided, interlocked strings play sweeping chords; small woods, set high, act as brilliant partials of upper brass. Timpani return; clashed cymbals mark start of phrases. Note that close-set bass chord of original is now set in open position. The grace note up-bow is followed by vigorous down-bow strokes on long notes. A perfect example of vivid sonority and powerful resonance simply realized. The contrast at bars 6 and 10 should be studied.

EXAMPLES

Several of the works already scored for string and wind ensembles should be set anew for full orchestra, using piano version. Compare scores with piano reductions of Classic and Romantic works originally composed for orchestra. The same with contemporary examples originally composed for piano, such as Ravel's *Mother Goose, Tzigane* (with solo violin) and *Tombeau de Couperin,* and Debussy's scoring of *Gymnopédie* by Satie. Compare, also, Weber's *Invitation to the Dance* with the scoring by Berlioz; note that the original key—D-flat—has been transposed to the more brilliant orchestral key of D major.

CHAPTER XVI

The Orchestral Painter

Our premise has been the kinship between painting and music, and in a wider sense the sympathy which draws together all the arts. Certainly there are deep-rooted affinities between music and architecture, poetry (language-plus-rhythm), dance, drama, and prose. An immutable point of difference is that of dimension. Music is (virtually) a temporal art; its companions are at once spatial and temporal.

Yet the spatial sense belongs in some degree to music; and here arises another correspondence between itself and the brother arts. Especially with orchestral music: a fine score is not conceived or performed as existing in one plane. It may be compared to a landscape, or a stage set. It has perspective—aerial suggestion—mutations of color; its objects and characters (themes, textures) are set in separate planes. A score should convey the sense of location —of proximity or distance. It must have atmosphere—the intangible which imparts lifelike character. And, like a picture, it has light and shade—what the artist calls *chiaroscuro*, the play of values.

The latter quality is finely described by George Moore in his book, *Modern Painting*, and his words deserve extended quotation:

By values is meant the amount of light and shade contained in a tone . . . . *Similar to a note in music,* no color can be said to be in itself either false or true, ugly or beautiful. *A note and a color acquire beauty and ugliness according to their associations;* therefore, to color well depends in the first instance on the painter's knowledge and intimate sense of contrast and similitude.

But there is another factor in the art of coloring as well; for just as the musician obtains richness and novelty of expression by means of the orchestra, so does the painter obtain depth and richness through a judicious distribution of values. . . . It is interesting and instructive to notice how those who seek the color without regard for the values inherent in the coloring matter, never succeed in producing more than a certain shallow superficial brilliancy; the color of such painters is never rich or profound, and although it may be beautiful, it is always wanting in the element of romantic charm and mystery.

The color is the melody, the values are the orchestration of the melody; and as the orchestration serves to enrich the melody, so do the values enrich the color. And as melody may—nay, must—exist if the orchestration be really beautiful, so color must inhere where the values have been finely observed. (Italics added.)

The reader will have remarked the insistent analogies between tone in painting and sound as an offspring of instruments.[1]

CONTEXT AS KEY TO COLOR

It follows as a corollary that context is a master key to color. A hue is heightened or subdued according to its location and associations. Placed against a quiet scheme, a single touch of brilliant color (or sound) acquires intensity; while in a pattern of high values the same stroke becomes diluted or neutralized. A trumpet heard amidst a sober scheme of middle strings stands forth boldly. In a powerful tutti the same timbre may be absorbed.

The influence of context is constant.[2] Instruments, like pigments, gain or lose effect according to their rôle in the total scheme. After an absence, instruments acquire new freshness and interest: this is one of the simplest and deepest principles of scoring. Vividness depends upon a fluid and varied play of timbres. Similar importance attaches to instrumental registers. No choir, color, or register should be exhausted through protracted use; this both for æsthetic reasons and for the sake of the players, especially those of wind instruments.

USE OF PERCUSSION

Percussion is a resource which needs sensitive control. Capable of affecting all surrounding means, these mobile instruments must be reserved for moments of greatest effect. Large percussions darken all textures; played strongly, they

[1] The following random extract, from Cheney's *World History of Art* (New York: Viking Press, 1937) illustrates anew the tendency among art critics to borrow the terms of music: "Titian is often described as the most musical of painters, and the adjective commonly used is 'symphonic.' The description is more than usually apt, particularly now when the moderns speak of formal orchestration as the basic virtue of great painting art. One might expect that when this great master had gone, Venice would have been left with composers of only a secondary and reflective genius—such indeed were a half-dozen decorators and portraitists who may be found in the museums. On the other hand there is another painter who, if not for all tastes the equal of Titian, is one of the Titans [Tintoretto]. He lacks the melodic clarity of the elder man, . . ." etc.

[2] As the great French critic Eugène Fromentin puts it: ". . . a color does not exist of itself, for it is modified, as we know, by the influence of a neighboring color. . . . Its quality comes to it from its surroundings—called also its complementaries."—*The Masters of Past Time* (London, Phaidon Press, Ltd. 1948).

blur or even overcome the lyric choirs, barring perhaps high brass. The drum colors range from delicate veiled grays to dense blacks. Small percussions add clear lights; they are trenchant, gay, and incisive. Used softly they strengthen and illumine the higher partials. Percussions afford unique border colors, enlarging the spheres of atmosphere and suggestion, and adding innumerable tints to the palette.

The effect of dynamics is pervasive throughout the orchestral process. These should be used with fine thought. Their effect upon the emotional scheme is immediate and decisive, while they engender subtleties comparable to the strokes and modulations of painting and sculpture.

COLOR PRIMARIES AND MIXTURES

There are three primary colors: red, yellow, and blue. Combined, they yield innumerable shades and tints. As they are mixed they lose purity, becoming increasingly opaque, ending at last in tones of gray.[3] Music has no precise counterpart for these hues, although for the sake of analogy we have employed the three lyric choirs (see Chapter I).

One of the cherished methods of painting, especially among the older masters, is known as glazing—the application of a transparent color film upon a solidly painted under-base (dead coloring). The effect is one of luminous mixture: the final color appears to be lighted from within, the whole suggesting a limpid stain. A comparable effect might be conveyed with instruments. Let us imagine a soft veil of divided string tone, sustained or tremolo, superimposed upon a harmonic choir of winds. According to the chosen dynamic scheme, the first or second group-qualities will act as the glazing medium. (If the points of the bows are used, greater transparency will result.) Such procedures are constantly employed by the sensitive orchestrator; consciously or not, he is using procedures akin to those of painting.

IMPRESSIONISM

We have seen that drawing, and in some cases design, arises as a product of polyphonic practice, and that this serves as the basis of most traditional scoring. Let us carry the analogy closer to the present by considering the tenets of Impressionism. Brief allusions have been made to the fresh vision and terse statement of Puccini and Stravinsky who, like other gifted program composers,

---

[3] At the opening of the *Russian Easter* Rimsky-Korsakoff places *in unison* all the woodwinds; perhaps to suggest a priestlike anonymity through this composite, paste-like color.

have devised imaginative means of applying tone. We shall describe briefly the principles followed by the late nineteenth-century painters banded together under the emblem of Impressionism.

Abandoning the academic practice of mixing colors on the palette, these French masters adopted the simple principle of juxtaposing or stippling on the canvas pure spots of natural color, following the principle of the prism and rainbow. Their god was light. Viewed at the right distance, the mixture of hues takes place in the eye—and mind—of the beholder. The procedure came to be known as *pointillisme* or divisionism and was practised sporadically before its systematic use in Paris. The intention was to avoid the impurity which results when pigments are rubbed together; in place of this the Impressionists sought the radiant vibrancy of optical blendings. (A certain price was paid by the more extreme exponents; objects and formal construction became subordinate to the sheer appeal of luminosity.)

And in attitude and results—as in period—there is a certain correspondence between the French symbolists, impressionist painters, and the fastidious school of composers led by Debussy.[4] Their tones are opalescent. They speak to the imagination. Suggestion rather than statement underlies their styles. Color is given the voice of poetry.

Many modern composers employ related methods. They choose unmixed timbres, place them at separate harmonic levels (pure colors set side by side), or they write rapid streams of tone which appear to blend. We devise a few simple examples of this process; in the first a rapid rhythmic grouping is divided among three woodwind types; while in the second the swift pace seems to fuse the running colors of flute and clarinet:

EXAMPLE 103

In the next example the growing string tone cuts off at the entrance of the trumpets; the colors are sharply broken; the device is related to that of substitution.

---

[4] It is also probable that the gauzy textures of Debussy suggest to many listeners the pearly tones of Corot's later manner or the tender surfaces of Renoir.

EXAMPLE 104

The following scheme shows the division of a figure between timpani and deep strings. It may be employed in any dynamic, conveying an effect of agitation:

EXAMPLE 105

The student can readily conceive of other examples based upon the deliberate opposition or alliance of timbres. Harmonic uses would comprise interlocking or superimposing of separate choirs, no tones being mixed.

Another application of *pointillisme* consists in the spot use of thematic fragments or motives; tiny strokes, like sparks of tone, moving swiftly through the picture (see Appendix).

Consideration of later painting styles—cubist, postimpressionist, Fauvist, expressionist, nonobjectivist, primitive, orientalist, surrealist—would take us too far afield. But it would be pointless to dispute their influence upon modern instrumental thought, although there is a debt on both sides.

COLOR AS EMOTIONAL VEHICLE

Composers, like painters, use color for its emotional as well as sensuous appeal. The timbre of each instrument has its own suggestion and association. This question is deeply affected by the character of the music and by the composer's personality and accent—by all that is represented by the word *style*.

Like a landscape at different seasons and at different hours, an instrumental voice is colored by immediate conditions. Its environment—harmony, dynamics, tempo, mood—joined with the curve and rhythm of melody, is the pervasive factor. It is well known that identical instruments—set in varying harmonic schemes—convey different impressions, although the melody may be the same.

Even more mysterious is the phenomenon which imparts a special feeling to the same instrument when used by different composers. Personality produces its own climate.

Nearly fifty years ago, Albert Schweitzer pointed out (what we should have known) an eloquent aspect of Bach's musical thought. He demonstrated that the master's music is a faithful commentary upon the text with which it deals. Even in the purely instrumental works, Bach is revealed as poet and painter as well as abstract architect. Indeed, he is now understood as a deeply subjective spirit. The same is true of Beethoven, acknowledged conqueror of musical forms. His Sixth Symphony is a nature fresco; the Fifth, a story of human travail; the Third, a hero's figure.

Let it be admitted: composers are painters—some of scenery, others of the soul. And every artist makes a portrait of himself.[5]

* * *

All of the examples that appear in the Appendix have been chosen to reveal the art of painting carried out in tone. It is hoped that they suggest how far music—the least concrete and factual of the arts—can convey characters, moods, and scenes with a subtlety which compensates for the precision enjoyed by the graphic and poetic arts.

[5] "In reality, the material in which the artist expresses himself is a secondary matter. He is not only a painter, or only a poet, or only a musician, but all in one. Various artists have their habitation in his soul." Albert Schweitzer, *J. S. Bach*, Vol. 2 (London: A. & C. Black, Ltd., 1923).

Codetta

Two centuries have passed since the death of Bach. The panorama of those years shows profound changes in the art of music. All of its elements are transformed (even transfigured), including the orchestra. Line and color have been brought into equilibrium. Science and sensibility have united to reshape instrumental expression.

An intensive study along historical lines could focus upon certain salient examples drawn from that crowded stage. As a concise study project, we present a group of twenty-five scores. Such a list does not embrace in all cases the highest productions of their composers or of the musical art; but the works are specimens of clear mastery chosen from Europe's schools.

CLASSIC-DRAMATIC
Gluck: Overture to *Alceste*

ARCHITECTURAL
Haydn: *Oxford* Symphony
Mozart: *Jupiter* Symphony
Beethoven: Seventh Symphony

ROMANTIC-DRAMATIC
Schubert: Eighth Symphony
Weber: *Freischütz* Overture
Berlioz: *Harold in Italy*
Liszt: *Faust* Symphony
Mendelssohn: *Scotch* Symphony
Brahms: *German Requiem*
Wagner: *Die Meistersinger*
Verdi: Requiem
Dvořák: Second Symphony
Strauss: *Ein Heldenleben*
Mahler: First Symphony
Sibelius: *Tapiola*
Elgar: *Falstaff*
Honegger: *King David*

COLORIST
Rimsky-Korsakoff: Suite, *Golden Cockerel*
Debussy: *La Mer*
Ravel: *Daphnis and Chloé*
Respighi: *Pines of Rome*

NEO-PRIMITIVE
Stravinsky: *Sacre du Printemps*

EXPRESSIONIST
Bartók: Music for Strings, Percussion, and Celesta
Prokofieff: Fifth Symphony

* * *

First and Last Things

Work for clear design. Line precedes color.

Work from large to small. Structure means breadth.

Work for solidity. But do not overload: a "white" score is not necessarily thin.

Respect details. Everything is important.

Resist formulas. Every score is a different work.

Write idiomatically. Instruments (like people) have their own accents.

A good idea is worth repeating. A bad one is worth nothing.

Consider tempo. Pace is all-important.

Rests: The windows of music. A score must breathe.

Dynamics deepen, as they create, mood.

Pianissimo is the leveling dynamic: it makes all things equal.

Color arises from context.

Fine values mean fine color.

Write for the ear, not the eye.

Sleek scoring is the hasheesh of Hollywood. It leaves an aftertaste.

Bad music has a long past, and a short future.

Vulgarity pleases the vulgar.

A perfect score contains a minimum of notes.

Lucidity: The sign of supreme workmanship.

Bibliography

ANDERSEN, Arthur Olaf, *Practical Orchestration* (Boston: C. C. Birchard & Co., 1929).

An elementary book devoted mainly to a description of the instruments, but containing useful advice on their combination and association from the harmonic viewpoint. Some of the material on instruments is outdated and unnecessarily restricted.

BERLIOZ-STRAUSS, *Treatise on Instrumentation,* trans. by Theodore Front (New York: E. F. Kalmus, 1948).

The French master's classic study was revised and enlarged by Richard Strauss in 1903. Berlioz is perhaps the most significant orchestral genius in the history of music. To praise his book is to gild fine gold. But the century that has elapsed since he wrote this work has brought important changes, especially among the wind instruments. Strauss deals with the latter by copious additions to the text and by numerous large-scale illustrations, many of these from the sources of Wagner. He also discusses some newer instruments and methods. By and large, the Straussian view is weighted on the side of German methods. Since the present work is nearly fifty years old, it lacks important examples of contemporary music. The translation is the first to offer this monumental work in English. It belongs in the library of every serious musician.

CARSE, Adam, *The History of Orchestration* (New York: E. P. Dutton & Co., Inc., 1925).

Authoritative within its compact scope; well designed and clearly set forth. It includes much valuable data on the earlier types of instruments and traces their physical evolution concisely. Highly useful in spite of the quarter century that has passed since its appearance.

———, *Orchestral Conducting* (London: Augener, Ltd., 1929).

Includes a brief description of the instruments together with an outline of the acoustics of the winds. Extremely concise; it is designed as a handbook.

COERNE, Louis Adolphe, *The Evolution of Modern Orchestration* (New York: The Macmillan Company, 1908).

A traditional presentation of its subject; the date of its production results in the omission of the contemporary school. The views are generally sound but unprovocative.

COLLINSON, Francis M., *Orchestration for the Theater* (London: John Lane, 1941).

This is the work of a skilled English practitioner; its precepts are adapted to the style of English theater music. The plan, purpose, and execution are clear and decisive.

FIDLER, Florence G., *A Handbook of Orchestration* (New York: E. P. Dutton & Co., Inc., 1921).

A handbook, devoted largely to a short description of the instruments. Contains much that is old and nothing that is new.

FORSYTH, Cecil, *Orchestration* (New York: The Macmillan Company, 1942).

This well-known work first appeared in 1914. After several reprintings, a revised edition was produced in 1935. Unfortunately, the present version contains few significant additions. Like many other books bearing the same title, the present work is misnamed; most of the material is devoted to the individual instruments; the book is more literally a compendium of the orchestral members. It has been widely used in England and this country, and its influence has been beneficial. The author is an Englishman who employs his language with urbanity and brilliance, which results in a work that is civilized and entertaining. The instruments described are those used in England, but their characteristics are in most cases identical with the American variety. Strangely lacking from the numerous illustrations are many famous contemporary names; among his compatriots Forsyth omits Holst, Walton, Bax, Bantock. On the other hand there appear six examples from the pen of Joseph Holbrooke, a nearly unknown composer. Certain material on the instruments is outdated.

GEVAERT, F. A., *New Treatise on Instrumentation; Course of Orchestration* (Paris: New York, Henry Lemoine, 1895).

These ample volumes form, with the Berlioz-Strauss and Rimsky-Korsakoff studies, the third member of the Big Three. They were completed in 1885 and 1890 respectively. The author was a distinguished Belgian savant. Composed on a lordly scale, the two tall volumes comprise together nearly 700 pages of text and illustrations, which disclose the virtues and deficiencies of the nineteenth-century viewpoint. Relatively few composers are quoted, but the given examples are broad enough to provide the necessary context (a merit shared by the Berlioz work). The music gives a fair picture of the classic, dramatic, and romantic styles. The instruments are discussed with authority and thoroughness, insofar as the period allows; thus, while a portion of the material is necessarily outmoded, the work as a whole will continue to command respect for its breadth and scholarly vision.

GUIRAUD, Ernest, *Traité Pratique d'Instrumentation*, revised and enlarged by Henri Büsser (Paris: Durand, 1933).

An excellent presentation from the French standpoint; compact, clear, and detailed. The author was a professor of composition at the Paris Conservatoire. M. Büsser's additions, which include numerous extracts from modern scores, greatly enlarge the book's value and heighten its contemporary flavor.

HEACOX, Arthur E., *Project Lessons in Orchestration* (Boston: Oliver Ditson Co., 1928).

This concise book is well designed for the beginning student, comprising a group of projects ranging from the scoring of a chorale to that of a cantata. The work is clearly laid out and expounded. But ideas have advanced since the work was written, some twenty years ago. A revised edition would be useful.

HENDERSON, W. J., *The Orchestra and Orchestral Music* (New York: Charles Scribner's Sons, 1923).

As its author remarks, "this is not a text book. It is not a treatise on instrumentation." The book is a succinct and penetrating review by the brilliant late music editor of the *New York Sun*. It is addressed to music lovers—an ample audience.

HOFFMAN, Richard, *Practical Instrumentation*, trans. by Robin H. Legge (New York: G. Schirmer, 1893).

This large-scale work is presented in seven parts, each dealing with chosen instrumental groups. The two-volume study is detailed and systematic, and is lavishly illustrated with examples in full score. Its viewpoint is that of the scholarly and well-trained musician of the German academy, *ca.* 1880. Inevitably, it is outweighted in the works and styles of the preceding century.

JACOB, Gordon, *Orchestral Technique* (London: Oxford University Press, 1931).

An excellent manual designed for the first-year student. The author is a well-known and highly equipped English teacher and composer. The views are sound and are admirably expressed. Especially valuable for its detailed study of the problems of arranging piano music for small and large orchestras. Extremely concise and well planned.

KLING, H., *Modern Orchestration and Instrumentation,* trans. by Gustav Saenger (New York: Carl Fischer, 1905).

Emphasis is laid on the individual instruments, including the rarer varieties. Despite its size, the book fails to deal with its subject in sufficient detail, and its author's views are decidedly old-fashioned. It is impossible to agree with certain statements, such as the ranges given for cello, trumpet, and harp. A section on the technique of conducting is included.

KOHS, Ellis B., *An Aural Approach to Orchestration* (New York: The Musical Mercury, 1940).

A brief and useful essay by one of the younger American composers. His thesis is defined by the book's title, and holds that the orchestra can only be studied practically through systematized listening. To this end he draws up a detailed list of examples from scores embracing the various instruments and their combinations, to be studied in conjunction with listed phonograph recordings. The flaw in this argument—and it is a serious one—is that recordings are unable to afford adequate acoustical results, regardless of the care and skill with which they are made; nor can phonographs—even the most elaborate—offer a suitable substitute for live performance. But all teachers recognize that recordings form a necessary *adjunct* to the study of orchestration.

LANGE, Arthur, *Arranging for the Modern Dance Orchestra* (New York: Arthur Lange, Inc., 1926).

The word *modern* must be seasoned with salt! Twenty-five years is very long in the world of dance and jazz. This is the work of a well-known and able professional. But to be completely useful, such a study would need revision every five years or so.

PARÈS, G., *Traité d'Instrumentation et d'Orchestration à l'usage de Musiques Militaires d'Harmonie et de Fanfare* (Paris: Henry Lemoine, 1898).

Despite its date, a work of unique value and thoroughness. Indispensable for those working in the field of wind instrument scoring. The work consists of two ample volumes, the second of which is devoted to examples.

PATTERSON, Frank, *Practical Instrumentation* (New York: G. Schirmer, 1923).

This book is made up of articles which originally appeared in the *Musical Courier*. It is designed for the autodidact. Emphasis is laid on the practical. One of the aims of the book is to explain the style favored by arrangers of "popular" music (thirty years ago). Strange companions are found among the composers cited: classicists cheek by jowl with ephemeral writers. The work is clear, within its own limits, but it suffers from the attempt to reduce and popularize a large, complex subject. Mozart's name occurs once; Beethoven's once; Haydn's not at all.

PROUT, Ebenezer, *The Orchestra* (London: Augener, Ltd., 1899).

The well-known English professor's work, in two volumes, has a curious dry fascination. But the wine has stood too long. Prout is the pure Victorian musician; patient, scrupulous, tradition-loving, and dull. In its long life this study of the orchestra and its instruments has been widely read. It has faded sadly—the fate of most studies of art techniques. Despite its antique dicta many composers of an earlier generation recall with nostalgia their Prout and its precise language.

RIMSKY-KORSAKOFF, Nicolas, *Principles of Orchestration* (Berlin, New York: Edition Russe de Musique, 1923).

This famous work has deeply influenced the course of modern scoring, particularly the style of the late French masters. Rimsky-Korsakoff was uniquely equipped to produce this work, the fruit of his ripest years. (It was written around the turn of the century.) He divides the orchestral problem into six sections, of which the most memorable and original is the one devoted to Harmony. More than 300 musical illustrations are employed in the work, all drawn from the author's own scores. This is perhaps the sole blemish—presenting as it does a single style and personality. The result, of course, is highly individual, at the expense of breadth and catholicity. The book, originally published in two volumes, was edited by its author's pupil, Maximilian Steinberg. It has been made available in a single volume reprint by E. F. Kalmus, trans. by Edward Agate (New York). The work as a whole must be considered as the bible of orchestral composers.

RUDOLF, Max, *The Grammar of Conducting* (New York: G. Schirmer, Inc., 1950).

A practical study of modern baton technique, up to date, clear, and systematic, by the gifted Metropolitan Opera conductor.

SACHS, Curt. *The History of Musical Instruments* (New York, W. W. Norton, 1940).

A comprehensive evolutionary study, which traces the instruments—including rare and obsolete types—from primitive times to the present day. Detailed and thorough.

SCHERCHEN, Hermann, *Handbook of Conducting* (London: Oxford University Press, 1933).

Although nearly twenty years old, Mr. Scherchen's work remains invaluable to the serious student and mature artist. Its material—original, sound, and penetrating—will be rewarding alike to the orchestral composer and conductor. The author is a distinguished European conductor, and a devoted champion of contemporary music. His views on the instruments, their use, and their possibilities for expression bear the marks of originality and authority. Particularly stimulating to the orchestrator is the section called "The Science of the Orchestra," which discusses the idiosyncrasies and subtleties of the instruments in a unique manner.

WELLESCZ, Egon E., *Die Neue Instrumentation* (Berlin: M. Hesse, 1929).

The two compact volumes deal with the latest instrumental ideas (up to the time of writing) and include a number of unusual examples which are not available in other texts, such as the music of Schönberg.

WIDOR, Ch-Marie, *The Technique of the Modern Orchestra*, trans. by Edward Suddard (London: Joseph Williams, Ltd., 1906).

As in the case of numerous other books, the title is misleading; Widor's book is mainly a compendium of the instruments. As such, and allowing for its age, it is clear and informative, and has value as a source of reference. A few inaccuracies, such as his description of the celesta, hardly impair its value. Widor was a famous organist, and he makes a spirited plea on behalf of his own instrument by way of rejoinder to Berlioz.

Appendix

NOTES ON THE EXAMPLES

1

Realism.—The Ride Through the Air; from Strauss's *Don Quixote*. Use of the wind machine. The pedal effect explains that the journey is purely imaginary; it holds the characters fast to earth.

2

Another example of literal painting, from the same score. The famous sheep scene. The bleating of the sheep is heard in flutter-tongued brass.

3

Calligraphy.—The monk Pimen writes the chronicles of Old Russia; cell scene from *Boris Godounov*. Subtle suggestion of contours of handwriting.

4

Pealing of Bells.—Association: suggestion through harmonies and colors. Coronation Scene from *Boris Godounov*.

5

Hallucination.—The same bells in ghostly echoes imagined by the conscience-tortured Tsar Boris.

6

Magic.—The charlatan animates his puppets: *Pétrouchka*.

7

The Supernatural.—Mist-like beginning of *L'Apprenti-Sorcier* of Paul Dukas.

8

The Macabre.—The "March to the Scaffold": *Fantastic* Symphony of Berlioz. Sodden colors.

9

Parody.—From the same work. Distortion of the "Beloved" motive. Stony textures. The "Witches' Sabbath."

10

Shifting Planes.—Another quotation from the Berlioz Symphony. Fourth movement.

11

Caricature.—Two Jews: one rich, one poor. Masterly drawings by Moussorgsky (*Pictures at an Exhibition*), scored by Ravel. (Portrait of *Goldenberg*.)

12

Impressionism.—Procession of Clouds: *Nuages* of Debussy. Evocative painting with slender means. Reed colors in parallel planes. Influence of Japanese wood prints—as in the pictures of Degas and Whistler.

13

Night Scene.—Tonal poetry. Suggestion through muted color-scale. "Perfumes of the Night" from *Iberia*. Delicate toning of all values. Woody timbres of xylophone.

14

Seascape.—Opening of Debussy's Suite *La Mer*. (Compare with original sketch reproduced in frontispiece.)

15

Miniature Painting.—Refinement and realism. Bird sounds beautifully suggested with a few touches. "Hop o' My Thumb" from Ravel's *Mother Goose*.

16

Association.—Sounds of the night (crickets' chirp) suggested by colors and rhythms of percussions and violins. Subdued doubling at twelfth of clarinet and piccolo. From the author's opera *The Warrior*.

17

Pointillism.—Icy tints scattered at various levels. Experiment in diffused timbres. Closing bars of "The Snow Queen" from the author's *Characters from Hans Christian Andersen* for small orchestra.

18

Exoticism.—Clanging Sonorities. Mixtures of pizzicato with woodwinds answered by very deep strings (pizzicato) plus piano and harp. Note strange blend at bar 4: curious composite of harp glissando and soft tam-tam. High, faint wood colors at bar 5 answered by buzzing percussions. From close of Stravinsky's *Song of the Nightingale*.

19

The Song of the Nightingale: Another version of the same story; by the present author. Closing page: Complex mixture of percussions, woods, and strings, to suggest tenuous, muffled colors of distant clock chimes. Faint, buzzing sonorities heard through polychords of muted strings, plus mixtures of dissonant celesta, harp harmonics, and deep bass pizzicati.

20

Portraiture.—Figure of the Astrologer: *Golden Cockerel* of Rimsky-Korsakoff. Pale, high colors; clear sounds of celesta. Opposition of gray timbres.

21

Power of the Triad.—Remotely related primary chords brilliantly placed for full chorus. Radiant, surging climax of Howard Hanson's *The Cherubic Hymn*. Scintillant doubling of voices by massed winds; strings grouped in dynamic ascents till measure 3, when they double first sopranos and altos. At this point suppression of timpani and Basses clarifies the huge sonority.

22

Merriment in Hell.—The "Pandemonium" from Berlioz's great dramatic legend. The triad again, now major—this time for infernal utterance. The composer—a good Frenchman—restricted his demon choir to men! The "new" language is his own concoction: when Berlioz needed something he invented it. Vehement rhythms from full orchestra, except deep strings, which play powerful, wailing figurations.

EXAMPLE 1 Strauss: *Don Quixote* (page 65)

EXAMPLE 2

Strauss: *Don Quixote* (page 33)

Example 3

Moussorgsky: *Boris Godounov* (page 86, large score)

EXAMPLE 4

Moussorgsky: *Boris Godounov* (page 212, large score)

EXAMPLE 5

Moussorgsky: *Boris Godounov* (page 632, large score)

EXAMPLE 6

Stravinsky: *Pétrouchka* (page 41)

EXAMPLE 7

Dukas: *Sorcerer's Apprentice* (page 1)

EXAMPLE 8

Berlioz: *Fantastic* Symphony (page 31)

Example 9

Berlioz: *Fantastic* Symphony (page 170)

EXAMPLE 10

Berlioz: *Fantastic* Symphony (page 156)

EXAMPLE 11

Moussorgsky-Ravel: *Pictures at an Exhibition* (page 65)

Example 12

Debussy: *Nuages* (page 1)

EXAMPLE 13

Debussy: Opening of "Perfumes of the Night" from *Iberia*

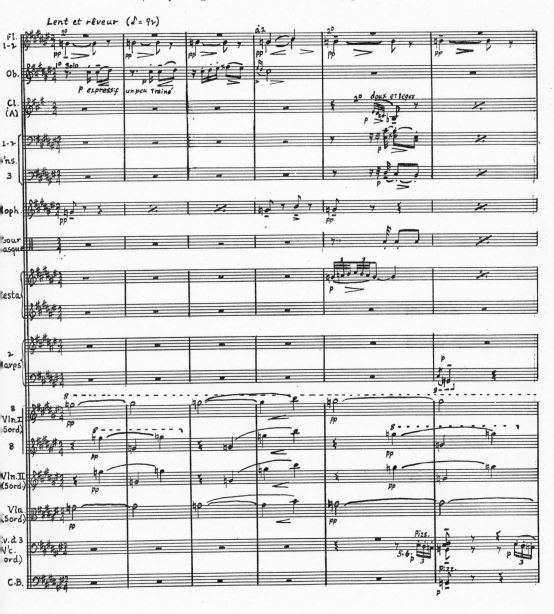

EXAMPLE 14

Debussy: *La Mer* (page 1)

EXAMPLE 15

Ravel: *Mother Goose* Suite (page 7)

EXAMPLE 16

Rogers: *The Warrior* (page 58)

EXAMPLE 17

Rogers: *The Snow Queen* (Characters after Andersen)

EXAMPLE 18

Stravinsky: *Song of the Nightingale* (last page)

EXAMPLE 19

Rogers: *Song of the Nightingale* (ending)

Example 20

Rimsky-Korsakoff: *The Golden Cockerel* (page 330, large score)

EXAMPLE 21

Howard Hanson: *Cherubic Hymn*

EXAMPLE 22

Berlioz: *Damnation of Faust* (page 370)

Index

(Compositions are listed under the composer's name.)